JUST LIKE JESUS

DEVOTIONAL

A Thirty-Day Walk with the Savior

Max Lucado

THOMAS NELSON
Since 1798

NASHVILLE   DALLAS   MEXICO CITY   RIO DE JANEIRO

Published in Nashville, Tennessee, by Thomas Nelson. Thomas Nelson is a registered trademark of Thomas Nelson, Inc.

Produced with the assistance of The Livingstone Corporation. Project staff includes Neil Wilson, Joyce Dinkins, Joan Guest, and Paige Drygas.

Thomas Nelson, Inc. titles may be purchased in bulk for educational, business, fund-raising, or sales promotional use. For information, please e-mail SpecialMarkets@ThomasNelson.com.

Unless otherwise noted, Scripture quotations are taken from the New Century Version®. © 2005 by Thomas Nelson, Inc. Used by permission. All rights reserved.

Other Scripture references are from the following sources: Holy Bible, New International Version®, NIV® (NIV). © 1973, 1978, 1984 by Biblica, Inc.™ Used by permission of Zondervan. All rights reserved worldwide. King James Version of the Bible (KJV). *The Living Bible* (TLB). © 1971. Used by permission of Tyndale House Publishers, Inc., Wheaton, Illinois 60189. All rights reserved. *The Message* by Eugene H. Peterson (MSG). © 1993, 1994, 1995, 1996, 2000. Used by permission of NavPress Publishing Group. All rights reserved. New King James Version® (NKJV). © 1982 by Thomas Nelson, Inc. Used by permission. All rights reserved. *J. B. Phillips: The New Testament in Modern English, Revised Edition* (PHILLIPS). © J. B. Phillips 1958, 1960, 1972. Used by permission of Macmillan Publishing Co., Inc. New American Standard Bible® (NASB). © The Lockman Foundation 1960, 1962, 1963, 1968, 1971, 1972, 1973, 1975, 1977. Used by permission. Revised Standard Version of the Bible (RSV). © 1946, 1952, 1971, 1973 by the Division of Christian Education of the National Council of the Churches of Christ in the U.S.A. Used by permission. *The Jerusalem Bible* (TJB). © 1966 by Darton, Longman & Todd Ltd. and Doubleday & Company, Inc. Used by permission. New Revised Standard Version of the Bible (NRSV). © 1989 by the Division of Christian Education of the National Council of the Churches of Christ in the U.S.A. All rights reserved. Today's English Version (TEV). © American Bible Society 1966, 1971, 1976, 1992. *Holy Bible*, New Living Translation (NLT), © 1996. Used by permission of Tyndale House Publishers, Inc., Wheaton, Illinois 60189. All rights reserved.

ISBN 978-0-8499-4850-3 (repackage)

Library of Congress has cataloged the earlier edition as follows:

Lucado, Max.
Just like Jesus devotional : a thirty day walk with the savior / by Max Lucado.
p. cm.
ISBN 978-0-8499-4400-0
1. Jesus Christ—Character—Prayer-books and devotions—English. 2. Devotional calendars. I. Title.
BT304 .L83 2003
242'.2—dc21   2002151121

Printed in the United States of America

20 21 PC/LSCH 10 9 8 7 6

INTRODUCTION

*W*hat if, for one day, Jesus were to become you? What if, for twenty-four hours, Jesus wakes up in your bed, walks in your shoes, lives in your house, assumes your schedule? Your boss becomes his boss, your mother becomes his mother, your pains become his pains. With one exception, nothing about your life changes. Your health doesn't change. Your circumstances don't change. Your schedule isn't altered. Your problems aren't solved. Only one change occurs.

What if, for one day, Jesus lives your life with his heart? Your heart gets the day off, and your life is led by the heart of Christ. His priorities govern your actions. His passions drive your decisions. His love directs your behavior.

What would you be like? Would people notice a change? Your family—would they see something new? Your coworkers—would they sense a difference? What about the less fortunate? Would you treat them the same? And your friends? Would they detect more joy? How about your enemies? Would they receive more mercy from Christ's heart than from yours?

And you? How would you feel? What alterations would this transplant have on your stress level? Your mood swings? Your temper? Would you sleep better? Would you see sunsets differently? Death differently? Taxes differently? Any chance you'd need fewer aspirin or sedatives? How about your reaction to traffic delays? (Ouch, that touched a nerve.) Would you still dread what you are dreading? Better yet, would you still do what you are doing?

Would you still do what you had planned to do for the next twenty-four hours? Pause and think about your schedule. Obligations. Engagements. Outings. Appointments. With Jesus taking over your heart, would anything change?

Keep working on this for a moment. Adjust the lens of your imagination until you have a clear picture of Jesus leading your life; then snap the shutter and frame the image. What you see is what God wants. He wants you to "think and act like Christ Jesus" (Phil. 2:5).

God's plan for you is nothing short of a new heart. If you were a car, God would want control of your engine. If you were a computer, God would claim the software and the hard drive. If you were an airplane, he'd take his seat in the cockpit. But you are a person, so God wants to change your heart.

Perhaps an instant makeover is a little too overwhelming. Let me invite you to join me for the next thirty days. We will be examining the heart of Jesus together. Since God's plan is to help us become more and more like his Son, it makes sense that we should spend time getting to know Jesus' heart. Because God wants to give you a heart like Jesus.

Let this mind be in you which was also in Christ Jesus.
—Philippians 2:5 NKJV

Just Like Jesus

God wants you to be just like Jesus. He wants you to have a heart like his.

I'm going to risk something here. It's dangerous to sum up grand truths in one statement, but I'm going to try. If a sentence or two could capture God's desire for each of us, it might read like this:

> God loves you just the way you are,
> but he refuses to leave you that way.
> *He wants you to be just like Jesus.*

God loves you just the way you are. If you think his love for you would be stronger if your faith were, you are wrong. If you think his love would be deeper if your thoughts were, wrong again. Don't confuse God's love with the love of people. The love of people often increases with performance and decreases with mistakes. Not so with God's love. He loves you right where you are. To quote my wife's favorite author:

> God's love never ceases. Never. Though we spurn him. Ignore him. Reject him. Despise him. Disobey

1

him. He will not change. Our evil cannot diminish his love. Our goodness cannot increase it. Our faith does not earn it any more than our stupidity jeopardizes it. God doesn't love us less if we fail or more if we succeed. God's love never ceases.*

God loves you just the way you are, but he refuses to leave you that way. When my daughter Jenna was a toddler, I used to take her to a park not far from our apartment. One day as she was playing in a sandbox, an ice-cream salesman approached us. I purchased her a treat, and when I turned to give it to her, I saw her mouth was full of sand. Where I intended to put a delicacy, she had put dirt.

Did I love her with dirt in her mouth? Absolutely. Was she any less my daughter with dirt in her mouth? Of course not. Was I going to allow her to keep the dirt in her mouth? No way. I loved her right where she was, but I refused to leave her there. I carried her over to the water fountain and washed out her mouth. Why? Because I love her.

God does the same for us. He holds us over the fountain. "Spit out the dirt, honey," our Father urges. "I have something better for you." And so he cleanses us of filth: immorality, dishonesty, prejudice, bitterness, greed. We don't enjoy the cleansing; sometimes we even opt for the dirt over the ice cream. "I can eat dirt if I want to!" we pout and proclaim. Which is true—we can. But if we do, the loss is ours. God has a better offer. He wants us to be just like Jesus.

---

* Adapted from Max Lucado, *A Gentle Thunder* (Nashville: Thomas Nelson, 1995), 46.

THINKING

When are you tempted to have "dirt" in place of "delicacy"?

What delicacy does God want to give you?

Why does God make such an amazing offer?

HEARING

Philippians 2:5–13 NIV:

> Your attitude should be the same as that of Christ Jesus:
>
> Who, being in very nature God,
>   did not consider equality with God something to
>   be grasped,
> but made himself nothing,
>   taking the very nature of a servant,
>   being made in human likeness.
> And being found in appearance as a man,
>   he humbled himself
>   and became obedient to death—
>   even death on a cross!
> Therefore God exalted him to the highest place
>   and gave him the name that is above every name,
> that at the name of Jesus every knee should bow,

in heaven and on earth and under the earth,
and every tongue confess that Jesus Christ is Lord,
to the glory of God the Father.

Therefore, my dear friends, as you have always obeyed—not only in my presence, but now much more in my absence—continue to work out your salvation with fear and trembling, for it is God who works in you to will and to act according to his good purpose.

REFLECTING

According to this passage, what does being like Jesus mean?

What did Jesus do for you?

How does that make you feel?

SPEAKING

Thank the Father for all he has done for you . . . be specific. Talk to him about the "dirt" and the "delicacy."

Give God permission to do whatever he decides to do in your life to make you more like Jesus.

*Take my yoke upon you and learn from me, for I am gentle
and humble in heart, and you will find rest for your souls.*
—Matthew 11:29 NIV

The Heart of Jesus

Jesus' heart was pure. The Savior was adored by thousands yet content to live a simple life. He was cared for by women (Luke 8:1–3) yet never accused of lustful thoughts, scorned by his own creation but willing to forgive them before they even requested his mercy. Peter, who traveled with Jesus for three and a half years, described him as a "lamb unblemished and spotless" (1 Peter 1:19 NASB). After spending the same amount of time with Jesus, John concluded, "And in him is no sin" (1 John 3:5 NIV).

Jesus' heart was peaceful. The disciples fretted over the need to feed the thousands, but not Jesus. He thanked God for the problem. The disciples shouted for fear in the storm, but not Jesus. He slept through it. Peter drew his sword to fight the soldiers, but not Jesus. He lifted his hand to heal. His heart was at peace. When his disciples abandoned him, did he pout and go home? When Peter denied him, did Jesus lose his temper? When the soldiers spit in his face, did he breathe fire in theirs? Far from it. He was at peace. He forgave them. He refused to be guided by vengeance. He also refused to be guided by anything other than his high call.

Jesus' heart was purposeful. Most lives aim at nothing in particular and achieve it. Jesus aimed at one goal—to save humanity from its sin. He could summarize his life with one sentence: "The Son of man came to seek and to save the lost" (Luke 19:10 RSV). Jesus was so focused on his task that he knew when to say, "My time has not yet come" (John 2:4) and when to say, "It is finished" (John 19:30). But he was not so focused on his goal that he was unpleasant.

Quite the contrary. How pleasant were his thoughts! Children couldn't resist Jesus. He could find beauty in lilies, joy in worship, and possibilities in problems. He would spend days with multitudes of sick people and still feel sorry for them. He spent more than three decades wading through the muck and mire of our sins yet still saw enough beauty in us to die for our mistakes.

But the crowning attribute of Christ was this: *his heart was spiritual.* His thoughts reflected his intimate relationship with the Father. "I am in the Father and the Father is in me," he stated (John 14:11). His first recorded sermon begins with the words, "THE SPIRIT OF THE LORD IS UPON ME" (Luke 4:18 NASB). He was "led by the Spirit" (Matt. 4:1 NIV) and "full of the Holy Spirit" (Luke 4:1 NIV). He returned from the desert "in the power of the Spirit" (Luke 4:14 NIV).

Jesus took his instructions from God. It was his habit to go to worship (Luke 4:16). It was his practice to memorize Scripture (Luke 4:4). Luke says Jesus "often slipped away to be alone so he could pray" (Luke 5:16). His times of prayer guided him. He once returned from prayer and announced it was time to move to another city (Mark 1:38). Another time of prayer resulted in the selection of the disciples (Luke 6:12–13). Jesus was led by an unseen hand. "The Son does whatever the

Father does" (John 5:19). In the same chapter he stated, "I can do nothing alone. I judge only the way I am told" (John 5:30). Jesus' heart was spiritual.

THINKING

What examples of Jesus' being "pure" can you remember?

Woman at the well

What example of Jesus' being "peaceful" is most meaningful to you?

Peter denied him 3x

What aspect of Jesus' heart do you most desire? Why?

peace - to be one + one w/ God

HEARING

Colossians 3:9–10 NKJV:

> Do not lie to one another, since you have put off the old man with his deeds, and have put on the new man who is renewed in knowledge according to the image of Him who created him.

REFLECTING

What are some evidences of the "old man"?

What evidence do you see in your life of the "new man"?

How do you know that God is transforming your heart to be like Jesus' heart?

SPEAKING

Thank your heavenly Father for giving you the heart of Jesus.

Ask God to show you specific areas in your life that require his special "renewing" attention.

The heart is deceitful above all things,
And desperately wicked;
Who can know it?
—Jeremiah 17:9 NKJV

The Heart of Humanity

O ur hearts seem so far from his. He is pure; we are greedy. He is peaceful; we are hassled. He is purposeful; we are distracted. He is pleasant; we are cranky. He is spiritual; we are earthbound. The distance between our hearts and his seems so immense. How could we ever hope to have the heart of Jesus?

Ready for a surprise? You already do. You already have the heart of Christ. Why are you looking at me that way? Would I kid you? If you are in Christ, you already have the heart of Christ. One of the supreme yet unrealized promises of God is simply this: if you have given your life to Jesus, Jesus has given himself to you. He has made your heart his home. It would be hard to say it more succinctly than Paul did: "Christ lives in me" (Gal. 2:20 MSG).

At the risk of repeating myself, let me repeat myself. If you have given your life to Jesus, Jesus has given himself to you. He has moved in and unpacked his bags and is ready to change you "into his likeness from one degree of glory to another" (2 Cor. 3:18 RSV). Paul explained it with these words: "Strange as it seems, we Christians actually do have within us a portion of the very thoughts and mind of Christ" (1 Cor. 2:16 TLB).

Strange is the word! If I have the mind of Jesus, why do I still think so much like me? If I have the heart of Christ, why do I still have the hang-ups of Max? If Jesus dwells within me, why do I still hate traffic jams?

Part of the answer is illustrated in a story about a lady who had a small house on the seashore of Ireland at the turn of the century. She was quite wealthy but also quite frugal. The people were surprised, then, when she decided to be among the first to have electricity in her home.

Several weeks after the installation, a meter reader appeared at her door. He asked if her electricity was working well, and she assured him it was. "I'm wondering if you can explain something to me," he said. "Your meter shows scarcely any usage. Are you using your power?"

"Certainly," she answered. "Each evening when the sun sets, I turn on my lights just long enough to light my candles; then I turn them off."*

She's tapped into the power but doesn't use it. Her house is connected but not altered. Don't we make the same mistake? We, too—with our souls saved but our hearts unchanged— are connected but not altered. Trusting Christ for salvation but resisting transformation. We occasionally flip the switch, but most of the time we settle for shadows.

What would happen if we left the light on? What would happen if we not only flipped the switch but lived in the light? What changes would occur if we set about the task of dwelling in the radiance of Christ?

---

* David Jeremiah, *The God of the Impossible*, audiotape.

No doubt about it: God has ambitious plans for us. The same one who saved your soul longs to remake your heart. His plan is nothing short of a total transformation: "He decided from the outset to shape the lives of those who love him along the same lines as the life of his Son" (Rom. 8:29 MSG).

THINKING

When do you seem to "live in the shadows"?

all in

What would it mean for you to "live in the light"?

pure, real

How does having the "mind of Christ" affect how you think and act?

what would Jesus do.

HEARING

2 Corinthians 3:16–18 NLT:

> But whenever anyone turns to the Lord, then the veil is taken away. Now, the Lord is the Spirit, and wherever the Spirit of the Lord is, he gives freedom. And all of us have had that veil removed so that we can be mirrors that brightly reflect the glory of the Lord. And as the Spirit of the Lord works within us, we become more and more like him and reflect his glory even more.

REFLECTING

Think back to when you came to faith in Christ. How did you know that the "veil" had been removed?

When do you most enjoy your freedom in Christ?

How do you know that Christ is living in you?

SPEAKING

Thank God for giving you a new mind, new sight, and true freedom.

Talk with God about those times when you've chosen to live in the shadows instead of the light.

Praise God for his transforming work in your heart.

*Having loved His own who were in the
world, He loved them to the end.*
—John 13:1 NKJV

The Constant Heart

Chances are you know the claustrophobia that comes with commitment. Pets are only the beginning. Instead of being reminded, "She is your dog," you're eventually told, "He is your husband." Or "She is your wife." Or "He is your child, parent, employee, boss, or roommate," or any other relationship that requires loyalty for survival.

Such permanence can lead to panic—at least it did in me. I had to answer some tough questions. Can I tolerate the same flat-nosed, hairy, hungry face every morning? (You wives know the feeling?) Am I going to be barked at until the day I die? (Any kids connecting here?) Will she ever learn to clean up her own mess? (Did I hear an "amen" from some parents?) Such are the questions we ask when we feel stuck with someone.

There is a word for this condition. Upon consulting the one-word medical dictionary (which I wrote the day before I crafted these thoughts), I discovered that this condition is a common malady known as *stuckititis*. (*Stuck* meaning "trapped." *Ititis* being the six letters you tag on to any word you want to sound impressive. Read it out loud: *stuckititis*.) *Max's Manual of Medical Terms* has this to say about the condition:

13

Attacks of *stuckititis* are limited to people who breathe and typically occur somewhere between birth and death. *Stuckititis* manifests itself in irritability, short fuses, and a mountain range of molehills. The common symptom of stuckititis victims is the repetition of questions beginning with *who*, *what*, and *why*. *Who* is this person? *What* was I thinking? *Why* didn't I listen to my mother?

This prestigious manual identifies three ways to cope with stuckititis: flee, fight, or forgive. Some opt to flee: to get out of the relationship and start again elsewhere, though they are often surprised when the condition surfaces on the other side of the fence as well. Others fight. Houses become combat zones, offices become boxing rings, and tension becomes a way of life. A few, however, discover another treatment: forgiveness. My manual has no model for how forgiveness occurs, but the Bible does.

Jesus himself knew the feeling of being stuck with someone. For three years he ran with the same crew. By and large, he saw the same dozen or so faces around the table, around the campfire, around the clock. They rode in the same boats and walked the same roads and visited the same houses, and I wonder, how did Jesus stay so devoted to his men? Not only did he have to put up with their visible oddities, he had to endure their invisible foibles. Think about it. He could hear their unspoken thoughts. He knew their private doubts. Not only that, he knew their future doubts. What if you knew every mistake your loved ones had ever made and every mistake they would ever make? What if you knew every thought they would have about you, every irritation, every dislike, every betrayal?

Was it hard for Jesus to love Peter, knowing Peter would someday curse him? Was it tough to trust Thomas, knowing Thomas would one day question Jesus' resurrection? How did Jesus resist the urge to recruit a new batch of followers? John wanted to destroy one enemy. Peter sliced off the ear of another. Just days before Jesus' death, his disciples were arguing about which of them was the best! How was he able to love people who were hard to like?

Few situations stir panic like being trapped in a relationship. It's one thing to be stuck with a puppy but something else entirely to be stuck in a marriage. We may chuckle over goofy terms like *stuckititis*, but for many, this is no laughing matter. For that reason I think it wise that we study Jesus' heart of forgiveness to understand what it means to be just like him. How was Jesus able to love his disciples?

THINKING
How does *stuckititis* feel in your life?

Back to that closing question: How *was* Jesus able to love his disciples? Think about this between now and your next reading.

Have you inflicted someone else with the condition *stuckititis*? In what relationships?

HEARING

1 Corinthians 13:4–7 NLT:

> Love is patient and kind. Love is not jealous or boastful or proud or rude. Love does not demand its own way. Love is not irritable, and it keeps no record of when it has been wronged. It is never glad about injustice but rejoices whenever the truth wins out. Love never gives up, never loses faith, is always hopeful, and endures through every circumstance.

REFLECTING

Which of the characteristics of love listed above can help someone overcome *stuckititis*? Why?

Which of the characteristics of love listed above has God been developing recently in your life?

Which of the characteristics of love listed above do you most long to sense as a trait in yourself?

SPEAKING

Turn those verses from 1 Corinthians 13 into a prayer by substituting your name each time the word *love* is used. Each time you find yourself saying something incongruent with who you actually are, ask God to transform you into a loving person.

Thank God for all the practical ways he has practiced his kind of love in your life, citing examples for each characteristic.

*If I then, your Lord and Teacher, have washed your feet,
you also ought to wash one another's feet. For I have given
you an example, that you should do as I have done to you.*
—John 13:14–15 NKJV

With Towel and Basin

*O*f all the times we see the bowing knees of Jesus, none
is so precious as when he kneels before his disciples
and washes their feet.

It was just before the Passover Feast. Jesus knew that
the time had come for him to leave this world and go
to the Father. Having loved his own who were in the
world, he now showed them the full extent of his love.
The evening meal was being served, and the devil
had already prompted Judas Iscariot, son of Simon, to
betray Jesus. Jesus knew that the Father had put all
things under his power, and that he had come from
God and was returning to God; so he got up from
the meal, took off his outer clothing . . . and began
to wash his disciples' feet, drying them with the towel
that was wrapped around him. (John 13:1–5 NIV)

It has been a long day. Jerusalem is packed with Passover
guests, most of whom clamor for a glimpse of the Teacher.

The spring sun is warm. The streets are dry. And the disciples are a long way from home. A splash of cool water would be refreshing.

The disciples enter, one by one, and take their places around the table. On the wall hangs a towel, and on the floor sit a pitcher and a basin. Any one of the disciples could volunteer for the job, but not one does.

After a few moments Jesus stands and removes his outer garment. He wraps a servant's girdle around his waist, takes up the basin, and kneels before one of the disciples. He unlaces a sandal and gently lifts the foot, places it in the basin, covers it with water, and begins to bathe it. One by one, one grimy foot after another, Jesus works his way down the row.

In Jesus' day the washing of feet was a task reserved not just for servants but for the lowest of servants. Every circle has its pecking order, and the circle of household workers was no exception. The servant at the bottom of the totem pole was expected to be the one on his knees with the towel and basin.

In this case the one with the towel and basin is the King of the universe. Hands that shaped the stars now wash away filth. Fingers that formed mountains now massage toes. And the One before whom all nations will one day kneel now kneels before his disciples. Hours before his own death, Jesus' concern is singular. He wants his disciples to know how much he loves them. More than removing dirt, Jesus is removing doubt.

Jesus knows what will happen to his hands at the crucifixion. Within twenty-four hours they will be pierced and lifeless. Of all the times we'd expect him to ask for the disciples' attention, this would be one. But he doesn't.

You can be sure Jesus knows the future of these feet he is washing. These twenty-four feet will not spend the next day following their master, defending his cause. These feet will dash for cover at the flash of a Roman sword. Only one pair of feet won't abandon him in the garden. One disciple won't desert him at Gethsemane—Judas won't even make it that far! He will abandon Jesus that very night at the table.

I looked for a Bible translation that reads, "Jesus washed all the disciples' feet except the feet of Judas," but I couldn't find one. What a passionate moment when Jesus silently lifts the feet of his betrayer and washes them in the basin! Within hours the feet of Judas, cleansed by the kindness of the one he will betray, will stand in Caiaphas's court.

Behold the gift Jesus gives his followers! He knows what these men are about to do. He knows they are about to perform the vilest act of their lives. By morning they will bury their heads in shame and look down at their feet in disgust. And when they do, he wants them to remember how his knees knelt before them and he washed their feet. He wants them to realize those feet are still clean. "You don't understand now what I am doing, but you will understand later" (John 13:7).

Remarkable. He forgave their sin before they even committed it. He offered mercy before they even sought it.

THINKING

How would you have responded if Jesus, knowing everything about you, knelt before you to wash your feet?

What's it like for you to experience forgiveness?

What's been the hardest aspect of giving and receiving forgiveness in your life?

HEARING
Matthew 6:12–15 NKJV:

> And forgive us our debts,
> As we forgive our debtors.
> And do not lead us into temptation,
> But deliver us from the evil one.
> For Yours is the kingdom and the power and the glory
>   forever. Amen.

> For if you forgive men their trespasses, your heavenly Father will also forgive you. But if you do not forgive men their trespasses, neither will your Father forgive your trespasses.

REFLECTING
Debts, sins, or trespasses—why did Jesus tell us to ask God to forgive us in the same way that we forgive others?

What actions similar to foot washing might we practice in someone else's life to express our forgiveness toward him or her?

Who needs forgiving in your life?

SPEAKING

Ask God to help you answer that last question truthfully. Write out a plan that will allow you to express forgiveness with some word or action.

Ask God to show you relationships in which you need to seek forgiveness. Determine what steps you will take to approach those persons.

Remember, the Lord forgave you, so you must forgive others.
—Colossians 3:13 NLT

The Forgiving Heart

*O**h, I could never do that*, you object. *The hurt is so deep. The wounds are so numerous. I can't forgive. Just seeing the person causes me to cringe.* Perhaps that is your problem. Perhaps you are seeing the wrong person or at least too much of the wrong person. Remember, the secret of being just like Jesus is "fixing our eyes" on him. Try shifting your glance away from the one who hurt you and setting your eyes on the one who has saved you.

Note the promise of John, "But if we live in the light, as God is in the light, we can share fellowship with each other. Then the blood of Jesus, God's Son, cleanses us from every sin" (1 John 1:7).

Aside from geography and chronology, our story is the same as the disciples'. We weren't in Jerusalem, and we weren't alive that night. But what Jesus did for them he has done for us. He has cleansed us. He has cleansed our hearts from sin.

Even more, he is still cleansing us! John tells us, "We are *being cleansed* from every sin by the blood of Jesus." In other words, we *are always being cleansed*. The cleansing is not a promise for the future but a reality in the present. Let a speck of dust fall on the soul of a saint, and it is washed away. Let a spot of filth land on the heart of God's child, and the filth is wiped away. Jesus still cleans his disciples' feet. Jesus still washes away stains. Jesus still purifies his people.

Our Savior kneels down and gazes upon the darkest acts of our lives. But rather than recoil in horror, he reaches out in kindness and says, "I can clean that if you want." And from the basin of his grace, he scoops a palm full of mercy and washes away our sin.

But that's not all he does. Because he lives in us, you and I can do the same. Because he has forgiven us, we can forgive others. Because he has a forgiving heart, we can have a forgiving heart. We can have a heart like his.

"If I, your Lord and Teacher, have washed your feet, you also should wash each other's feet. I did this as an example so that you should do as I have done for you" (John 13:14–15).

Jesus washes our feet for two reasons. The first is to give us mercy; the second is to give us a message, and that message is simply this: Jesus offers unconditional grace; we are to offer unconditional grace. The mercy of Christ preceded our mistakes; our mercy must precede the mistakes of others. Those in the circle of Christ had no doubt of his love; those in our circles should have no doubts about ours.

What does it mean to have a heart like his? It means to kneel as Jesus knelt, touching the grimy parts of the people we are stuck with and washing away their unkindnesses with kindness. Or as Paul wrote, "Be kind and loving to each other, and forgive each other just as God forgave you in Christ" (Eph. 4:32).

"But, Max," you are saying, "I've done nothing wrong. I'm not the one who cheated. I'm not the one who lied. I'm not the guilty party here." Perhaps you aren't. But neither was Jesus.

Of all the men in that room, only one was worthy of having his feet washed. And he was the one who washed the feet. The one worthy of being served, served others. The genius of Jesus' example is that the burden of bridge-building falls on the strong one, not on the weak one. The one who is innocent is the one who makes the gesture.

And you know what happens? More often than not, if the one in the right volunteers to wash the feet of the one in the wrong, both parties get on their knees. Don't we all think we are right? Hence we wash each other's feet. Please understand: *relationships don't thrive because the guilty are punished but because the innocent are merciful.*

THE POWER OF FORGIVENESS

Recently I shared a meal with some friends. A husband and wife wanted to tell me about a storm they were weathering. Through a series of events, she learned of an act of infidelity that had occurred over a decade ago. He had made the mistake of thinking it'd be better not to tell her, so he didn't. But she found out. And as you can imagine, she was deeply hurt.

Through the advice of a counselor, the couple dropped everything and went away for several days. A decision had to be made. Would they flee, fight, or forgive? So they prayed. They talked. They walked. They reflected. In this case the wife was clearly in the right. She could have left. Women have done so for lesser reasons. Or she could have stayed and made his life a living hell. Other women have done that. But she chose a different response.

On the tenth night of their trip, my friend found a card on his pillow. On the card was a printed verse: "I'd rather do nothing with you than something without you." Beneath the verse she had written these words:

I forgive you. I love you. Let's move on.

The card might as well have been a basin. And the pen might as well have been a pitcher of water, for out of it poured pure mercy, and with it she washed her husband's feet.

Certain conflicts can be resolved only with a basin of water. Are any relationships in your world thirsty for mercy? Are there any sitting around your table who need to be assured of your grace? Jesus made sure his disciples had no reason to doubt his love. Why don't you do the same?

THINKING

Allow the idea of forgiveness to settle in your soul for a moment. What does it cost to forgive like the examples above?

Read that last paragraph again. How did you answer Max's last question? ("Why don't you do the same?")

If hurts are part of life's negative unfairness, how is forgiveness part of life's positive unfairness?

HEARING

Romans 5:6–8 NKJV:

> For when we were still without strength, in due time Christ died for the ungodly. For scarcely for a righteous man will one die; yet perhaps for a good man someone would even dare to die. But God demonstrates His own love toward us, in that while we were still sinners, Christ died for us.

REFLECTING

Why do you think forgiveness feels so much like dying?

How have you responded to the fact that Christ's death for you demonstrated God's love for you?

Thinking back over the last three readings on forgiveness, what specific action would most clearly indicate that you have understood deeply what it means to be forgiven by God?

SPEAKING

Reference 1 John 1:9 as you pray about the condition of forgiveness in your heart. Bring your relationship with God up-to-date today by confessing unsettled matters between you and the Lord.

Ask God for a courageous soul as you consider people in your life whom you may have to forgive and those from whom you may have to ask forgiveness.

And behold, a leper came and worshiped Him, saying,
"Lord, if You are willing, You can make me clean."
—Matthew 8:2 NKJV

Looking for Compassion

Sometimes my curiosity gets the best of me, and I wonder out loud. That's what I'm about to do here—wonder out loud about a man who feels Jesus' compassionate touch. He makes one appearance, has one request, and receives one touch. But that one touch changes his life forever. And I wonder if his story went something like this:

For five years no one touched me. No one. Not one person. Not my wife. Not my child. Not my friends. No one touched me. They saw me. They spoke to me. I sensed love in their voices. I saw concern in their eyes. But I didn't feel their touch. There was no touch. Not once. No one touched me.

What is common to you, I coveted. Handshakes. Warm embraces. A tap on the shoulder to get my attention. A kiss on the lips to steal a heart. Such moments were taken from my world. No one touched me. No one bumped into me. What I would have given to be bumped into, to be caught in a crowd, for my shoulder to brush against another's. But for five years it has not happened. How could it? I was not allowed on the streets. Even the rabbis kept their distance from me. I was not permitted in my synagogue. Not even welcome in my own house.

I was untouchable. I was a leper. And no one touched me. Until today.

I wonder about this man because in New Testament times leprosy was the most dreaded disease. The condition rendered the body a mass of ulcers and decay. Fingers would curl and gnarl. Blotches of skin would discolor and stink. Certain types of leprosy would numb nerve endings, leading to a loss of fingers, toes, even a whole foot or hand. Leprosy was death by inches.

The social consequences were as severe as the physical. Considered contagious, the leper was quarantined, banished to a leper colony. In Scripture the leper is symbolic of the ultimate outcast: infected by a condition he did not seek, rejected by those he knew, avoided by people he did not know, condemned to a future he could not bear. And in the memory of each outcast must have been the day he was forced to face the truth: life would never be the same.

One year during harvest my grip on the scythe seemed weak. The tips of my fingers numbed. First one finger then another. Within a short time I could grip the tool but scarcely feel it. By the end of the season, I felt nothing at all. The hand grasping the handle might as well have belonged to someone else—the feeling was gone. I said nothing to my wife, but I know she suspected some-

thing. How could she not? I carried my hand against my body like a wounded bird.

One afternoon I plunged my hands into a basin of water intending to wash my face. The water reddened. My finger was bleeding, bleeding freely. I didn't even know I was wounded. How did I cut myself? On a knife? Did my hand slide across the sharp edge of metal? It must have, but I didn't feel anything.

"It's on your clothes too," my wife said softly. She was behind me. Before looking at her, I looked down at the crimson spots on my robe. For the longest time I stood over the basin, staring at my hand. Somehow I knew my life was being forever altered.

"Shall I go with you to tell the priest?" she asked.

"No," I sighed. "I'll go alone."

I turned and looked into her moist eyes. Standing next to her was our three-year-old daughter. Squatting, I gazed into her face and stroked her cheek, saying nothing. What could I say? I stood and looked again at my wife. She touched my shoulder, and with my good hand, I touched hers. It would be our final touch.

Five years have passed, and no one has touched me since, until today.

The priest didn't touch me. He looked at my hand, now wrapped in a rag. He looked at my face, now shadowed in sorrow. I've never faulted him for what he said. He was only doing as he was instructed. He covered his mouth and extended his hand, palm forward. "You are unclean," he told me. With one pronouncement I lost my family, my farm, my future, my friends.

My wife met me at the city gates with a sack of

clothing and bread and coins. She didn't speak. By now friends had gathered. What I saw in their eyes was a precursor to what I've seen in every eye since: fearful pity. As I stepped out, they stepped back. Their horror of my disease was greater than their concern for my heart—so they, and everyone else I have seen since, stepped back.

The banishing of a leper seems harsh, unnecessary. The Ancient East hasn't been the only culture to isolate their wounded, however. We may not build colonies or cover our mouths in their presence, but we certainly build walls and duck our eyes. And a person needn't have leprosy to feel quarantined.

THINKING
In what situations in life have you felt "quarantined"?

Putting yourself in the rags of the leper, what specific response to your disease would be hardest to accept?

What aspect of human contact would create the deepest longing in you?

HEARING
Hebrews 4:14–16 NKJV:

> Seeing then that we have a great High Priest who
> has passed through the heavens, Jesus the Son of
> God, let us hold fast our confession. For we do not
> have a High Priest who cannot sympathize with our
> weaknesses, but was in all points tempted as we are,
> yet without sin. Let us therefore come boldly to the
> throne of grace, that we may obtain mercy and find
> grace to help in time of need.

REFLECTING
How have your "quarantine" experiences affected your
thoughts and attitudes toward God?

Based on the verses above, how well does God understand
what you are going through?

Why does God tell us that he "sympathizes with our
weaknesses"?

SPEAKING

Tell God one thing that frustrates you and one thing that helps you in knowing that he understands what you go through.

Ask God to help you "come boldly to the throne of grace, that we may obtain mercy and find grace to help in time of need."

Then Jesus put out His hand and touched him, saying, "I am willing; be cleansed." Immediately his leprosy was cleansed.
—Matthew 8:3 NKJV

The Compassionate Heart

*T*he leper continues his story:

> *Several weeks ago I dared walk the road to my village. I had no intent of entering. Heaven knows I only wanted to look again upon my fields. Gaze again upon my home. And see, perchance, the face of my wife. I did not see her. But I saw some children playing in a pasture. I hid behind a tree and watched them scamper and run. Their faces were so joyful and their laughter so contagious that for a moment, for just a moment, I was no longer a leper. I was a farmer. I was a father. I was a man.*
>
> *Infused with their happiness, I stepped out from behind the tree, straightened my back, breathed deeply . . . and they saw me. Before I could retreat, they saw me. And they screamed. And they scattered. One lingered, though, behind the others. One paused and looked in my direction. I don't know, and I can't say for sure, but I think, I really think, she was my daughter. And I don't know, I really can't say for sure. But I think she was looking for her father.*

That look is what made me take the step I took today. Of course it was reckless. Of course it was risky. But what did I have to lose? He calls himself God's Son. Either he will hear my complaint and kill me or accept my demands and heal me. *Those were my thoughts. I came to him as a defiant man. Moved not by faith but by a desperate anger. God had wrought this calamity on my body and he would either fix it or end it.*

But then I saw him, and when I saw him, I was changed. You must remember, I'm a farmer, not a poet, so I cannot find the words to describe what I saw. All I can say is that the Judean mornings are sometimes so fresh and the sunrises so glorious that to look at them is to forget the heat of the day before and the hurt of times past. When I looked at his face, I saw a Judean morning.

Before he spoke, I knew he cared. Somehow I knew he hated this disease as much as—no, more than—I hate it. My rage became trust, and my anger became hope. From behind a rock, I watched him descend a hill. Throngs of people followed him. I waited until he was only paces from me, then I stepped out. "Master!"

He stopped and looked in my direction as did dozens of others. A flood of fear swept across the crowd. Arms flew in front of faces. Children ducked behind parents. "Unclean!" someone shouted. Again, I don't blame them. I was a huddled mass of death. But I scarcely heard them. I scarcely saw them. Their panic I'd seen a thousand times. His compassion, however, I'd never beheld. Everyone stepped back except him. He stepped toward me. Toward me.

Five years ago my wife had stepped toward me. She was the last to do so. Now he did. I did not move. I just spoke. "Lord, you can heal me if you will." Had he healed me with a word, I would have been thrilled. Had he cured me with a prayer, I would have rejoiced. But he wasn't satisfied with speaking to me. He drew near me. He touched me. Five years ago my wife had touched me. No one had touched me since. Until today.

"I will." His words were as tender as his touch. "Be healed!"

Energy flooded my body like water through a furrowed field. In an instant, in a moment, I felt warmth where there had been numbness. I felt strength where there had been atrophy. My back straightened, and my head lifted. Where I had been eye level with his belt, I now stood eye level with his face. His smiling face.

He cupped his hands on my cheeks and drew me so near I could feel the warmth of his breath and see the wetness in his eyes. "Don't tell anyone about this. But go and show yourself to the priest and offer the gift Moses commanded for people who are made well. This will show the people what I have done."

And so that is where I am going. I will show myself to my priest and embrace him. I will show myself to my wife, and I will embrace her. I will pick up my daughter, and I will embrace her. And I will never forget the one who dared to touch me. He could have healed me with a word. But he wanted to do more than heal me. He wanted to honor me, to validate me, to christen me. Imagine that . . . unworthy of the touch of a man yet worthy of the touch of God.

The Power of the Godly Touch

The touch did not heal the disease, you know. Matthew is careful to mention that it was the pronouncement and not the touch of Christ that cured the condition. "Jesus reached out his hand and touched the man and said, 'I will. Be healed!' And immediately the man was healed from his disease" (Matt. 8:3).

The infection was banished by a word from Jesus. The loneliness, however, was treated by a touch from Jesus.

Oh, the power of a godly touch. Haven't you known it? The doctor who treated you, or the teacher who dried your tears?

Was there a hand holding yours at a funeral? Another on your shoulder during a trial? A handshake of welcome at a new job? A pastoral prayer for healing? Haven't we known the power of a godly touch?

Can't we offer the same?

Perhaps you already do. You may have the master touch of the Physician himself. You use your hands to pray over the sick and minister to the weak. If you aren't touching them personally, your hands are writing letters, dialing phones, baking pies. You have learned the power of a touch.

But others of us tend to forget. Our hearts are good; it's just that our memories are bad. We forget how significant one touch can be. We fear saying the wrong thing or using the wrong tone or acting the wrong way. So rather than do it incorrectly, we do nothing at all.

Aren't we glad Jesus didn't make the same mistake? If your fear of doing the wrong thing prevents you from doing anything, keep in mind the perspective of the lepers of the world. They aren't picky. They aren't finicky. They're just lonely. They are yearning for a godly touch.

Jesus touched the untouchables of the world. Will you do the same?

THINKING
When have you felt that amazing power of a compassionate touch?

In what ways has Jesus responded to the "untouchable" areas in your life?

What occasions can you recall in which you were able to offer a compassionate touch to someone in need?

HEARING
Colossians 3:11–13 NIV:

> Here there is no Greek or Jew, circumcised or uncircumcised, barbarian, Scythian, slave or free, but Christ is all, and is in all.
>
> Therefore, as God's chosen people, holy and dearly loved, clothe yourselves with compassion, kindness, humility, gentleness and patience. Bear with each other and forgive whatever grievances you may have against one another. Forgive as the Lord forgave you.

REFLECTING

If a child asked you to explain that phrase, "clothe yourselves with compassion," what would you say?

What people in your life have come closest to fitting that description, "clothed with compassion"?

What do you feel God would need to add or take away from your life in order to make you more compassionate like Jesus?

SPEAKING

Ask God for a special alertness to sense moments in this day when you can clothe yourself with compassion, kindness, humility, gentleness, and patience.

Thank the Lord for each person who has demonstrated one of those character traits of Jesus in your life.

Do not let this Book of the Law depart from your mouth; meditate on it day and night, so that you may be careful to do everything written in it. Then you will be prosperous and successful.
—Joshua 1:8 NIV

Listening to God's Heart

*E*quipped with the right tools, we can learn to listen to God. What are those tools? Here are the ones I have found helpful.

A regular time and place. Select a slot on your schedule and a corner of your world, and claim it for God. For some it may be best to do this in the morning. "In the morning my prayer comes before you" (Ps. 88:13 NIV). Others prefer the evening and agree with David's prayer: "Let my . . . praise [be] like the evening sacrifice" (Ps. 141:2). Others prefer many encounters during the day. Apparently the author of Psalm 55 did. He wrote, "Evening, morning and noon I cry out" (v. 17 NIV).

Some sit under a tree, others in the kitchen. Maybe your commute to work or your lunch break would be appropriate. Find a time and place that seems right for you.

How much time should you take? As much as you need. Value quality over length. Your time with God should last long enough for you to say what you want and for God to say what he wants.

Which leads us to a second tool you need—*an open Bible.*

God speaks to us through his Word. The first step in reading the Bible is to ask God to help you understand it. "But the Helper will teach you everything and will cause you to remember all that I told you. This Helper is the Holy Spirit whom the Father will send in my name" (John 14:26).

Before reading the Bible, pray. Don't go to Scripture looking for your own idea; go searching for God's. Read the Bible prayerfully. Also, read the Bible carefully. Jesus told us, "Search, and you will find" (Matt. 7:7). God commends those who "chew on Scripture day and night" (Ps. 1:2 MSG). The Bible is not a newspaper to be skimmed but rather a mine to be quarried. "Search for it like silver, and hunt for it like hidden treasure. Then you will understand respect for the LORD, and you will find that you know God" (Prov. 2:4–5).

Here is a practical point. Study the Bible a little at a time. God seems to send messages as he did his manna: one day's portion at a time. He provides "A command here, a command there. A rule here, a rule there. A little lesson here, a little lesson there" (Isa. 28:10). Choose depth over quantity. Read until a verse "hits" you, then stop and meditate on it. Copy the verse onto a sheet of paper, or write it in your journal, and reflect on it several times.

On the morning I wrote this, for example, my quiet time found me in Matthew 18. I was only four verses into the chapter when I read, "The greatest person in the kingdom of heaven is the one who makes himself humble like this child" (v. 4). I needed to go no further. I copied the words in my journal and have pondered them on and off during the day. Several times I asked God, "How can I be more childlike?" By the end of the day, I was reminded of my tendency to hurry and my proclivity to worry.

Will I learn what God intends? If I listen, I will.

Don't be discouraged if your reading reaps a small harvest. Some days a lesser portion is all we need. A little girl returned from her first day at school. Her mom asked, "Did you learn anything?" "I guess not," the girl responded. "I have to go back tomorrow and the next day and the next day . . ."

Such is the case with learning. And such is the case with Bible study. Understanding comes a little at a time over a lifetime.

There is a third tool for having a productive time with God. Not only do we need a regular time and place and an open Bible, we also need *a listening heart.* Don't forget the admonition from James: "The man who looks into the perfect mirror of God's law, the law of liberty, and makes a habit of so doing, is not the man who sees and forgets. He puts that law into practice and he wins true happiness" (James 1:25 PHILLIPS).

We know we are listening to God when what we read in the Bible is what others see in our lives. It's one thing not to know. It's another to know and not learn. Paul urged his readers to put into practice what they had learned from him. "What you have learned and received and heard and seen in me, do" (Phil. 4:9 RSV).

If you want to be just like Jesus, let God have you. Spend time listening for him until you receive your lesson for the day—then apply it.

THINKING

How will you know when you are practicing "a listening heart"?

What time and place seems the best for you to spend alone with God on a regular basis?

How would you describe the present depth of awareness of God in your life, and how would you like that awareness to change in the next few months?

HEARING

Jeremiah 29:12–13 NASB:

> Then you will call upon Me and come and pray to Me, and I will listen to you. You will seek Me and find Me when you search for Me with all your heart.

REFLECTING

Notice the actions in these verses: "call upon Me," "come," "pray to Me," and "search for Me with all your heart." How do you understand each of these actions?

How does your soul respond to the two promises in these verses: "I will listen to you," and "you will find Me"?

How do the three tools mentioned (time/place, open Bible, listening heart) affect God's conditional words in these verses—"when you search for Me with all your heart"?

SPEAKING
During the next few days, make it a point to stop and listen for a while before you read this devotional or your Bible. Ask God to help you listen for him. Do the same each time you finish reading.

Make a note below or in a notebook of the thoughts God brings to mind as you are listening for him. You don't want to forget what God says to you.

*But blessed are your eyes for they see, and your ears for
they hear; for assuredly, I say to you that many prophets
and righteous men desired to see what you see, and did not
see it, and to hear what you hear, and did not hear it.*
—Matthew 13:16–17 NKJV

Hearing God's Music

I'd like to tell you a story you've heard before, though
you've not heard it as I am going to tell it. But you have
heard it. Surely you have, for you are in it. You are one of the
characters. It is the story of the dancers who had no music.

Can you imagine how hard that would be? Dancing with
no music? Day after day they came to the great hall just off
the corner of Main and Broadway. They brought their wives.
They brought their husbands. They brought their children
and their hopes. They came to dance.

The hall was prepared for a dance. Streamers strung,
punch bowls filled. Chairs were placed against the walls.
People arrived and sat, knowing they had come to a dance
but not knowing how to dance because they had no music.
They had balloons; they had cake. They even had a stage on
which the musicians could play, but they had no musicians.

One time a lanky fellow claimed to be a musician. He
sure looked the part, what with his belly-length beard and
fancy violin. He stood before them and pulled the violin

out of the case and placed it beneath his chin. *Now we will dance*, they thought, but they were wrong. For though he had a violin, his violin had no strings. The pushing and pulling of his bow sounded like the creaking of an unoiled door. Who can dance to a sound like that? So the dancers took their seats again.

Some tried to dance without the music. One wife convinced her husband to give it a try, so out on the floor they stepped, she dancing her way and he dancing his. Both efforts were commendable—but far from compatible. He danced some form of partnerless tango, while she was spinning like a ballerina. A few tried to follow their cue, but since there was no cue, they didn't know how to follow. The result was a dozen or so dancers with no music, going this way and that, bumping into each other and causing more than one observer to seek safety behind a chair.

Over time, however, those dancers grew weary, and everyone resumed the task of sitting and staring and wondering if anything was ever going to happen. And then one day it did.

Not everyone saw him enter. Only a few. Nothing about his appearance would compel your attention. His looks were common, but his music was not. He began to sing a song, soft and sweet, kind and compelling. His song took the chill out of the air and brought a summer-sunset glow to the heart.

And as he sang, people stood—a few at first, then many—and they began to dance. Together. Flowing to a music they had never heard before, they danced.

Some, however, remained seated. What kind of musician is this who never mounts the stage? Who brings no band? Who has no costume? Why, musicians don't just walk in off the street. They have an entourage, a reputation, a persona to project and protect. Why, this fellow scarcely mentioned his name!

"How can we know what you sing is actually music?" they challenged.

His reply was to the point: "Let the man who has ears to hear use them."

But the nondancers refused to hear. So they refused to dance. Many still refuse. The musician comes and sings. Some dance. Some don't. Some find music for life; others live in silence. To those who miss the music, the musician gives the same appeal: "Let the man who has ears to hear use them."

THINKING
What does Jesus' music sound like to you?

Where do you fit in the story just told?

How have you most often responded to Jesus' invitation to dance?

HEARING
Zephaniah 3:17 NIV:

> The LORD your God is with you,
>   he is mighty to save.

He will take great delight in you,
    he will quiet you with his love,
    he will rejoice over you with singing.

REFLECTING

Who is the audience and who is the performer in this verse?

How would it affect you to hear God whisper to you, "I delight in you"?

Based solely on this verse, what would God include in his songs about you?

SPEAKING

Take a few moments to express to God your appreciation for his love for you.

Respond audibly to the fact that God has said to you, "I delight in you."

No one can see God, but Jesus Christ is exactly like him.
He ranks higher than everything that has been made.
—Colossians 1:15

God's Translator

*J*esus' relationship with God went far deeper than a
daily appointment. Our Savior was always aware of his
Father's presence. Listen to his words:

> The Son can do nothing on his own, but only what
> he sees the Father doing; for whatever the Father
> does, the Son does likewise. (John 5:19 NRSV)

> I can do nothing on my own. As I hear, I judge.
> (John 5:30 NRSV)

> I am in the Father and the Father is in me. (John
> 14:11 NRSV)

Clearly, Jesus didn't act unless he saw his Father act. He
didn't judge until he heard his Father judge. No act or deed
occurred without his Father's guidance. His words have the
ring of a translator.

There were a few occasions in Brazil when I served as a
translator for an English speaker. He stood before the audience,

complete with the message. I stood at his side, equipped with the language. My job was to convey his story to the listeners. I did my best to allow his words to come through me. I was not at liberty to embellish or subtract. When the speaker gestured, I gestured. As his volume increased, so did mine. When he got quiet, I did too.

When he walked this earth, Jesus was "translating" God all the time. When God got louder, Jesus got louder. When God gestured, Jesus gestured. He was so in sync with the Father that he could declare, "I am in the Father and the Father is in me" (John 14:11 NRSV). It was as if he heard a voice others were missing.

I witnessed something similar to this on an airplane once. I kept hearing outbursts of laughter. The flight was turbulent and bumpy, hardly a reason for humor. But some fellow behind me was cracking up. No one else, just him. Finally I turned to see what was so funny. He was wearing headphones and apparently listening to a comedian. Because he could hear what I couldn't, he acted differently than I did.

The same was true with Jesus. Because he could hear what others couldn't, he acted differently than they did. Remember when everyone was troubled about the man born blind? Jesus wasn't. Somehow he knew that the blindness would reveal God's power (John 9:3). Remember when everyone was distraught about Lazarus's illness? Jesus wasn't. Rather than hurry to his friend's bedside, he said, "This sickness will not end in death. It is for the glory of God, to bring glory to the Son of God" (John 11:4). It was as if Jesus could hear what no one else could. How could a relationship be more intimate? Jesus had unbroken communion with his Father.

Do you suppose the Father desires the same for us?

Absolutely. Paul wrote that we have been "predestined to be conformed to the image of his Son" (Rom. 8:29 NRSV). Let me remind you: God loves you just the way you are, but he refuses to leave you that way. He wants you to be just like Jesus. God desires the same abiding intimacy with you that he had with his Son.

THINKING

Describe the two or three most powerful emotions you connect with the idea of intimacy with God.

What person do you know who most clearly represents for you someone who listens to God more than he or she pays attention to what the world is shouting?

Which experience with God would you like to be able to translate for the world if they would listen?

HEARING

1 John 1:3:

> We announce to you what we have seen and heard, because we want you also to have fellowship with us. Our fellowship is with God the Father and with his Son, Jesus Christ.

REFLECTING

As the apostle John put it, there's a relationship between what we have experienced and what we can share with others. What have you "seen and heard" about Jesus that you feel compelled to translate for others?

How have shared experiences with Christ affected your relationships with others? To what degree has "fellowship" been a by-product?

What does it mean to you to have fellowship with God the Father and God the Son?

SPEAKING

Focus on the moments in the last day when you were aware of God's presence, and thank him for revealing himself to you.

Think of several situations you expect to experience in the next day or two, and ask the Lord to make you aware of his unwavering companionship.

Even if I walk through a very dark valley, I will
not be afraid, because you are with me.
—Psalm 23:4

The Intimate Heart

God draws several pictures to describe the relationship he envisions. *One is of a vine and a branch.*

"I am the vine, and you are the branches. If any remain in me and I remain in them, they produce much fruit. But without me they can do nothing. . . . If you remain in me and follow my teachings, you can ask anything you want, and it will be given to you." (John 15:5, 7)

God wants to be as close to us as a branch is to a vine. One is an extension of the other. It's impossible to tell where one starts and the other ends. The branch isn't connected only at the moment of bearing fruit. The gardener doesn't keep the branches in a box and then, on the day he wants grapes, glue them to the vine. No, the branch constantly draws nutrition from the vine. Separation means certain death.

God also uses the temple to depict the intimacy he desires. "Don't you know," Paul wrote, "that your body is the temple of the Holy Spirit, who lives in you and was given to you by

God?" (1 Cor. 6:19 TEV). Think with me about the temple for a moment. Was God a visitor or a resident in Solomon's temple? Would you describe his presence as occasional or permanent? You know the answer. God didn't come and go, appear and disappear. He was a permanent presence, always available.

What incredibly good news for us! We are *never* away from God! He is *never* away from us—not even for a moment! God doesn't come to us on Sunday mornings and then exit on Sunday afternoons. He remains within us, continually present in our lives.

The biblical analogy of marriage is the third picture of this encouraging truth. Aren't we the bride of Christ (Rev. 21:2)? Aren't we united with him (Rom. 6:5 RSV)? Haven't we made vows to him, and hasn't he made vows to us?

What does our marriage to Jesus imply about his desire to commune with us? For one thing, the communication never stops. In a happy home the husband doesn't talk to the wife only when he wants something from her. He doesn't pop in just when he wants a good meal or a clean shirt or a little romance. If he does, the home is not a home—it's a brothel that serves food and cleans clothes.

Healthy marriages have a sense of "remaining." The husband remains in the wife, and she remains in him. There is a tenderness, an honesty, an ongoing communication. The same is true in our relationship with God. Sometimes we go to him with our joys, and sometimes we go with our hurts, but we always go. And as we go, the more we go, the more we become like him. Paul wrote we are being changed from "glory to glory" (2 Cor. 3:18 KJV).

People who live long lives together eventually begin to

sound alike, to talk alike, even to think alike. As we walk with God, we take on his thoughts, his principles, his attitudes. We take on his heart.

And just as in marriage, communion with God is no burden. Indeed, it is a delight. "How lovely is your dwelling place, O Lord Almighty! My soul yearns, even faints, for the courts of the Lord; my heart and my flesh cry out for the living God" (Ps. 84:1–2 NIV). The level of communication is so sweet that nothing compares with it.

THINKING

How do you relate emotionally to each of the three biblical pictures of intimacy with God—vine/branches, temple/dweller, and marriage?

Which one of those most clearly describes your present experience of intimacy with God?

Which one of those represents an aspect of your relationship with God that needs attention?

HEARING

Psalm 139:2–6 MSG:

> I'm an open book to you;
>> even from a distance, you know what I'm thinking.
> You know when I leave and when I get back;
>> I'm never out of your sight.
> You know everything I'm going to say
>> before I start the first sentence.
> I look behind me and you're there,
>> then up ahead and you're there, too—
>> your reassuring presence, coming and going.
> This is too much, too wonderful—
>> I can't take it all in!

REFLECTING

Is being "an open book" to God primarily an exciting, confusing, delightful, fearful, challenging, or other kind of experience for you?

What would God expect from us if he is our constant companion?

If it's true, as David exclaimed, that we "can't take it all
in," in what ways have you found yourself taking in more
intimacy with God than you did, say, five years ago?

SPEAKING

Compose three statements you can say to the Lord that summarize how you feel about his intimate relationship with you.

Express your gratitude for the insights God has given you
as you've asked him to make your heart like Jesus' heart.

Every morning, I tell you what I need,
and I wait for your answer.
—Psalm 5:3

Practicing Intimacy

*H*ow, then, do I live in God's presence? How do I detect his unseen hand on my shoulder and his inaudible voice in my ear? A sheep grows familiar with the voice of the shepherd. How can you and I grow familiar with the voice of God? Here are a few ideas:

Give God your waking thoughts. Before you face the day, face the Father. Before you step out of bed, step into his presence. I have a friend who makes it a habit to roll out of his bed onto his knees and begin his day in prayer. Personally, I don't get that far. With my head still on the pillow and my eyes still closed, I offer God the first seconds of my day. The prayer is not lengthy and far from formal. Depending on how much sleep I got, it may not even be intelligible. Often it's nothing more than: "Thank you for a night's rest. I belong to you today."

C. S. Lewis wrote: "The moment you wake up each morning . . . [all] your wishes and hopes for the day rush at you like wild animals. And the first job of each morning consists in shoving them all back; in listening to that other voice, taking that other point of view, letting that other, larger, stronger, quieter life come flowing in."*

Here is how the psalmist began his day: "Every morning, I tell you what I need, and I wait for your answer" (Ps. 5:3).

Which leads to the second idea:

Give God your waiting thoughts. Spend time with him in silence. The mature married couple has learned the treasure of shared silence; they don't need to fill the air with constant chatter. Just being together is sufficient. Try being silent with God. "Be still, and know that I am God" (Ps. 46:10 NIV). Awareness of God is a fruit of stillness before God.

Dan Rather once asked Mother Teresa, "What do you say to God when you pray?"

Mother Teresa answered quietly, "I listen."

Taken aback, Rather tried again. "Well, then, what does God say?"

Mother Teresa smiled. "He listens."

Give God your whispering thoughts. Through the centuries Christians have learned the value of brief sentence prayers, prayers that can be whispered anywhere, in any setting. Frank Laubach sought unbroken communion with God by asking him questions. Every two or three minutes he would pray, "Am I in your will, Lord? Am I pleasing you, Lord?"

In the nineteenth century an anonymous Russian monk set out to live in unceasing communion with God. In a book titled *The Way of the Pilgrim,* he tells of how he learned to have one prayer constantly in his mind: "Lord Jesus Christ, Son

---

* As quoted in Timothy Jones, *The Art of Prayer* (New York: Ballantine Books, 1997), 133.

of God, have mercy on me, a sinner." With time, the prayer became so internalized that he was constantly praying it, even while consciously occupied with something else.

Imagine considering every moment as a potential time of communion with God. By the time your life is over, you will have spent six months at stoplights, eight months opening junk mail, a year and a half looking for lost stuff (double that number in my case), and a whopping five years standing in various lines.*

Why don't you give these moments to God? By giving God your whispering thoughts, the common becomes uncommon. Simple phrases such as "Thank you, Father," "Be sovereign in this hour, O Lord," and "You are my resting place, Jesus" can turn a commute into a pilgrimage. You needn't leave your office or kneel in your kitchen. Just pray where you are. Let the kitchen become a cathedral or the classroom a chapel. Give God your whispering thoughts.

And last, give God your waning thoughts. At the end of the day, let your mind settle on him. Conclude the day as you began it: talking to God. Thank him for the good parts. Question him about the hard parts. Seek his mercy. Seek his strength. And as you close your eyes, take assurance in the promise: "He who watches over Israel will neither slumber nor sleep" (Ps. 121: 4 NIV). If you fall asleep as you pray, don't worry. What better place to doze off than in the arms of your Father?

---

* Charles R. Swindoll, *The Finishing Touch* (Dallas: Word Publishing, 1994), 292.

THINKING

What places and regular events in your life might be candidates for transformation into times with God?

When was the last time you fell asleep praying?

Waking, waiting, whispering, and waning thoughts—which of these could benefit from more practice of intimacy with God?

HEARING

John 17:23:

> "I will be in them and you will be in me so that they will be completely one. Then the world will know that you sent me and that you loved them just as much as you loved me."

REFLECTING

Practicing intimacy shares similarities with practicing medicine. The term implies a foundation of knowledge that improves through experience. How has your practice of intimacy with God developed in the last few years?

In what situations and occasions are you most deeply aware of Christ's presence "in you" as he promised?

To what degree have you consciously invited Jesus to be more and more at home in your heart?

SPEAKING

Thank God for the thrilling opportunity to practice intimacy with him.

Talk to another believer this next week about his or her experiences in practicing intimacy with God.

*And all of us have had that veil removed so that we can
be mirrors that brightly reflect the glory of the Lord. And
as the Spirit of the Lord works within us, we become more
and more like him and reflect his glory even more.*
—2 Corinthians 3:18 NLT

A Worship-Hungry Heart

*D*iscover the purpose of worship—to change the face
of the worshiper. This is exactly what happened to
Christ on the mountain. Jesus' appearance was changed:
"His face became bright like the sun" (Matt. 17:2).

The connection between the face and worship is more
than coincidental. Our faces are the most public parts of our
bodies, covered less than any other area. They are also the
most recognizable parts of our bodies. We don't fill a school
annual with photos of people's feet but rather with photos
of faces. God desires to take our faces, these exposed and
memorable parts of our bodies, and use them to reflect his
goodness. Paul wrote: "Our faces, then, are not covered. We
all show the Lord's glory, and we are being changed to be
like him. This change in us brings ever greater glory, which
comes from the Lord, who is the Spirit" (2 Cor. 3:18).

God invites us to see his face so he can change ours. He
uses our uncovered faces to display his glory. The transformation isn't easy. The sculptor of Mount Rushmore faced

a lesser challenge than does God. But our Lord is up to the task. He loves to change the faces of his children. By his fingers, wrinkles of worry are rubbed away. Shadows of shame and doubt become portraits of grace and trust. He relaxes clenched jaws and smoothes furrowed brows. His touch can remove the bags of exhaustion from beneath the eyes and turn tears of despair into tears of peace.

How? Through worship.

We'd expect something more complicated, more demanding. A forty-day fast or the memorization of Leviticus perhaps. No. God's plan is simpler. He changes our faces through worship.

Exactly what is worship? I like King David's definition. "O magnify the LORD with me, and let us exalt His name together" (Ps. 34:3 NASB). Worship is the act of magnifying God. Enlarging our vision of him. Stepping into the cockpit to see where he sits and observe how he works. Of course, his size doesn't change, but our perception of him does. As we draw nearer, he seems larger. Isn't that what we need? A big view of God? Don't we have big problems, big worries, big questions? Of course we do. Hence we need a big view of God.

Worship offers that. How can we sing "Holy, Holy, Holy" and not have our vision expanded? Or what about these lines from "It Is Well with My Soul"?

My sin—O the bliss of this glorious thought,
My sin, not in part but the whole,
Is nailed to the cross and I bear it no more,
Praise the Lord, praise the Lord, O my soul!

(Horatio Spafford)

Can we sing those words and not have our countenance illuminated?

A vibrant, shining face is the mark of one who has stood in God's presence. After speaking to God, Moses had to cover his face with a veil (Ex. 34:33–35). After seeing heaven, Stephen's face glowed like that of an angel (Acts 6:15).

God is in the business of changing the face of the world.

Let me be very clear. This change is his job, not ours. Our goal is not to make our faces radiant. Not even Jesus did that. Matthew says that Jesus "was transfigured" not "Jesus changed his appearance" (Matt. 17:2 NIV). Moses didn't even know his face was shining (Ex. 34:29). Our goal is not to conjure up some fake, frozen expression. Our goal is simply to stand before God with a prepared and willing heart and then let God do his work.

And he does. He wipes away the tears. He mops away the perspiration. He softens our furrowed brows. He touches our cheeks. He changes our faces as we worship.

But there's more. Not only does God change the face of those who worship; he changes those who watch us worship.

THINKING

If someone accompanied you to church next week and simply watched your face the whole time, what would they report about the way you worship?

When you think about Jesus, how would you describe the look on his face?

How does the way Jesus looks at you affect the way you look at him?

HEARING
Acts 2:25–26 MSG:

> "I saw God before me for all time.
>   Nothing can shake me; he's right by my side.
> I'm glad from the inside out, ecstatic;
>   I've pitched my tent in the land of hope."

REFLECTING
To what degree does the word *gladness* apply to your experience of worship?

How do you prepare for worship? What do you want to express to God as you gather with other believers?

In what ways can you practice a more intentional awareness that others may be affected by the way you worship—your children, your spouse, other Christians, and even nonbelievers?

SPEAKING

Ask God for the same capacity David had to "see him before you for all time." Thank him for what he has already revealed of himself to you.

What single action (humming a hymn, speaking a verse, choosing to smile, and so forth) would communicate best to others your anticipation of gladness the next time you enter God's house?

Enter into His gates with thanksgiving,
And into His courts with praise.
Be thankful to Him, and bless His name.
—Psalm 100:4 NKJV

The Heart of Worship

*A*n amazing dynamic occurs when we come to worship with a heart of worship. Paul told the Corinthian church to worship in such a clear way that if an unbeliever entered, "he would find . . . the secrets of his heart revealed; and so he would fall down on his face and worship God, declaring that God is indeed among you" (1 Cor. 14:24–25 TJB).

David cited the evangelistic power of honest worship: "He put a new song in my mouth, a song of praise to our God. Many people will see this and worship him. Then they will trust the LORD" (Ps. 40:3).

Your heartfelt worship is a missionary appeal. Let unbelievers hear the passion of your voice or see the sincerity in your face, and they may be changed. Peter was. When Peter saw the worship of Jesus, he said, "Lord, it is good that we are here. If you want, I will put up three tents here—one for you, one for Moses, and one for Elijah" (Matt. 17:4).

Mark says Peter spoke out of fear (9:6). Luke says Peter spoke out of ignorance (9:33). But whatever the reason, at least Peter spoke. He wanted to do something for God. He didn't understand that God wants hearts and not tents, but at least he was moved to give something.

Why? Because he saw the transfigured face of Christ. The same happens in churches today. When people see us giving heartfelt praise to God—when they hear our worship—they are intrigued. They want to see who's in charge! Sparks from our fire tend to ignite dry hearts.

I experienced something similar in Brazil. Our house was only blocks away from the largest soccer stadium in the world. At least once a week Maracana stadium would be packed with screaming soccer fans. Initially I was not numbered among them, but their enthusiasm was contagious. I wanted to see what they were so excited about. By the time I left Rio, I was a soccer convert and could shout with the best of them.

Seekers may not understand all that happens in a house of worship. They may not understand the meaning of a song or the significance of the communion, but they know joy when they see it. And when they see your face changed, they may want to see God's face.

By the way, wouldn't the opposite be equally true? What happens when a seeker sees boredom on your face? Others are worshiping and you are scowling? Others are in his presence, but you are in your own little world? Others are seeking God's face while you are seeking the face of your wristwatch?

As long as I'm getting personal, may I come a step closer? Parents, what are your children learning from your worship? Do they see the same excitement as when you go to a basketball game? Do they see you prepare for worship as you do for a vacation? Do they see you hungry to arrive, seeking the face of the Father? Or do they see you content to leave the way you came?

They are watching. Believe me. They are watching.

Do you come to church with a worship-hungry heart? Our Savior did.

May I urge you to be just like Jesus? Prepare your heart for worship. Let God change your face through worship. Demonstrate the power of worship. Above all, seek the face of the One in charge. Those who see Christ find their faces changed! The same can happen to you.

THINKING

Look through the above paragraphs and answer the probing questions that appear there.

What would it mean for you to come to church with a worship-hungry heart?

In what ways do you think worship (which we give to God) is also beneficial for us?

HEARING

Psalm 34:4–7 NLT:

> I prayed to the LORD, and he answered me,
>> freeing me from all my fears.
> Those who look to him for help will be radiant with joy;

no shadow of shame will darken their faces.
I cried out to the LORD in my suffering, and he heard me.
He set me free from all my fears.
For the angel of the LORD guards all who fear him,
and he rescues them.

REFLECTING

For the full effect, read the rest of Psalm 34. What reasons
does the psalmist give for his joy?

What are the two contrasting ways he uses the word *fear* in
this passage?

What characteristic of God would you like others to see
when they look at your face?

SPEAKING

Adapt and expand the following prayer as you practice being
more prepared for worship: *Lord, rewrite my face so people can
read good things about you when they look at me.*

Write out Psalm 122:1 on a slip of paper and put it where
you will see it on your way to church. "I was happy when they
said to me, 'Let's go to the Temple of the LORD.'"

*I don't mean to say that I have already achieved these
things or that I have already reached perfection! But I
keep working toward that day when I will finally be all
that Christ Jesus saved me for and wants me to be.*
—Philippians 3:12 NLT

The Heart on Target

Life is tough enough as it is. It's even tougher when we're
headed in the wrong direction.

One of the incredible abilities of Jesus was to stay on
target. His life never got off track. Not once do we find him
walking down the wrong side of the fairway. He had no
money, no computers, no jets, no administrative assistants or
staff. Yet Jesus did what many of us fail to do. He kept his life
on course.

As Jesus looked across the horizon of his future, he could
see many targets. Many flags were flapping in the wind, each
of which he could have pursued. He could have been a politi-
cal revolutionary. He could have been a national leader. He
could have been content to be a teacher and educate minds or
to be a physician and heal bodies. But in the end he chose to
be a Savior and save souls.

Anyone near Christ for any length of time heard it from
Jesus himself. "The Son of Man came to find lost people and
save them" (Luke 19:10). "The Son of Man did not come to

be served. He came to serve others and to give his life as a ransom for many people" (Mark 10:45).

The heart of Christ was relentlessly focused on one task. The day he left the carpentry shop of Nazareth he had one ultimate aim: the cross of Calvary. He was so focused that his final words before he died were, "It is finished" (John 19:30).

How could Jesus say he was finished? There were still the hungry to feed, the sick to heal, the untaught to instruct, and the unloved to love. How could he say he was finished? Simple. He had completed his designated task. His commission was fulfilled. The painter could set aside his brush, the sculptor lay down his chisel, the writer put away his pen. The job was done.

Wouldn't you love to be able to say the same? Wouldn't you love to look back on your life and know you had done what you were called to do?

Our lives tend to be so scattered. We're intrigued by one trend only until the next comes along. Suckers for the latest craze or quick fix. This project, then another. Lives with no strategy, no goal, no defining priority. Playing the holes out of order. Erratic. Hesitant. Living life with the hiccups. We are easily distracted by the small things and forget the big things. I saw an example of this the other day in the grocery store.

There is one section in the supermarket where I am a seasoned veteran: the sample section. I'm never one to pass up a snack. Last Saturday I went to the back of the store where the samplers tend to linger. Bingo! There were two sample givers awaiting hungry sample takers. One had a skillet of sausage and the other a plate full of cream cheese–covered celery. You'll be proud to know I opted for the celery. I wanted the sausage, but I knew the celery was better for me.

Unfortunately the celery lady never saw me. She was too

busy straightening her sticks. I walked past her, and she never looked up. The sausage lady, however, saw me coming and extended the plate. I declined and made another circle past the celery lady. Same response. She never saw me. She was too busy getting her plate in order. So I made another loop past the sausage lady. Once again the offer came, and once again with admirable resolve I resisted. I was committed to doing the right thing.

So was the celery lady. She was determined to get every celery stick just so on her plate. But she cared more about the appearance of her product than the distribution. I stopped. I coughed. I cleared my throat. I did everything but sing a song. Still no response. The sausage lady, however, was waiting on me with sizzling sausage. I gave in; I ate the sausage.

The celery lady got off target. She was so occupied with the small matters (i.e., celery organization) that she forgot her assignment (i.e., to help needy, hungry, pitiful shoppers like me).

How do we keep from making the same mistake in life? God wants us to be just like Jesus and have focused hearts.

THINKING
What parts of life tend to distract your heart the most?

When God walks through your life, does he find you more like the celery lady or the sausage lady?

What is the one project, effort, or dream about which you would most like to be able to say someday, "It is finished"?

HEARING
2 Timothy 4:7–8 NKJV:

> I have fought the good fight, I have finished the race, I have kept the faith. Finally, there is laid up for me the crown of righteousness, which the Lord, the righteous Judge, will give to me on that Day, and not to me only but also to all who have loved His appearing.

REFLECTING
How would you describe the "fight" or the "race" that your life represents?

In tomorrow's reading, you will find some specific help in staying on target. What resources have you discovered to keep your heart on target?

When you read the phrase "laid up for me the crown of righteousness, which the Lord . . . will give to me," what kind of anticipation do you feel?

SPEAKING

Think of people you know who could use some encouragement in their "fight" or "race." Pray for them and then find a way to let them know you're pulling for them.

Thank the Lord for those things that remind you of your target. Give God your full permission to continue to train you for special service.

The heart is deceitful above all things
and beyond cure.
Who can understand it?
—Jeremiah 17:9 NIV

Four Heart Questions

*H*ow do I stay on target? Consulting the map would be
a good start. What's true on the golf course is true in
life as well. I save myself a lot of hassle when I take enough
time to look at the map on the scorecard. The course archi-
tects draw one for easily confused duffers like me. The one
who designed our life-course left us directions.

By answering four simple questions, we can be more like
Jesus; we can stay on course with our lives.

Romans 8:28 says, "We know that all that happens to us
is working for our good if we love God and are fitting into his
plans" (TLB). The first step for focusing your heart is to ask
this question: Am I fitting into God's plan?

God's plan is to save his children. "He does not want anyone to be destroyed, but wants all to turn away from their sins"
(2 Peter 3:9 TEV).

If God's goal is the salvation of the world, then my goal
should be the same. The details will differ from person to
person, but the big picture is identical for all of us. "We're
Christ's representatives. God uses us to persuade men and

women" (2 Cor. 5:20 MSG). Regardless of what you don't know about your future, one thing is certain: you are intended to contribute to the good plan of God, to tell others about the God who loves them and longs to bring them home.

But exactly how are you to contribute? What is your specific assignment? Let's seek the answer with a second question: What are my longings?

This question may surprise you. Perhaps you thought your longings had nothing to do with keeping your life on track. I couldn't disagree more. Your heart is crucial. Psalm 37:4 says, "Enjoy serving the LORD, and he will give you what you want." When we submit to God's plans, we can trust our desires. Our assignment is found at the intersection of God's plan and our pleasures. *What do you love to do? What brings you joy? What gives you a sense of satisfaction?*

Some long to feed the poor. Others enjoy leading the church. Others relish singing or teaching or holding the hands of the sick or counseling the confused. Each of us has been made to serve God in a unique way.

> For we are God's workmanship, created in Christ Jesus to do good works, which God prepared in advance for us to do. (Eph. 2:10 NIV)

> You made all the delicate, inner parts of my body, and knit them together in my mother's womb. . . . Your workmanship is marvelous. . . . You were there while I was being formed in utter seclusion! You saw me before I was born and scheduled each day of my life before I began to breathe. (Ps. 139:13–16 TLB)

You are a custom design; you are tailor-made. God prescribed your birth. Regardless of the circumstances that surrounded your arrival, you are not an accident. God planned you before you were born.

The longings of your heart, then, are not incidental; they are critical messages. The desires of your heart are not to be ignored; they are to be consulted. As the wind turns the weather vane, so God uses your passions to turn your life. God is too gracious to ask you to do something you hate.

Be careful, however. Don't consider your desires without considering your skills. Move quickly to the third question: What are my abilities?

There are some things we want to do but simply aren't equipped to accomplish. I, for example, have the desire to sing. Singing for others would give me wonderful satisfaction. The problem is, it wouldn't give the same satisfaction to my audience. I am what you might call a prison singer—I never have the key, and I'm always behind a few bars.

Paul gave good advice in Romans 12:3: "Have a sane estimate of your capabilities" (PHILLIPS).

In other words, be aware of your strengths. When you teach, do people listen? When you lead, do people follow? When you administer, do things improve? Where are you most productive? Identify your strengths, and then—this is important—major in them. Take a few irons out of the fire so this one can get hot. Failing to focus on our strengths may prevent us from accomplishing the unique tasks God has called us to do.

A lighthouse keeper who worked on a rocky stretch of coastline received oil once a month to keep his light burning. Not being far from a village, he had frequent guests. One night a woman needed oil to keep her family warm. Another night a father needed oil for his lamp. Then another needed oil to lubricate a wheel. All the requests seemed legitimate, so the lighthouse keeper tried to meet them all. Toward the end of the month, however, he ran out of oil, and his lighthouse went dark, causing several ships to crash on the coastline. The man was reproved by his superiors. "You were given the oil for one reason," they said, "to keep the light burning."

We cannot meet every need in the world. We cannot please every person in the world. We cannot satisfy every request in the world. But some of us try. And in the end, we run out of fuel. Have a sane estimate of your abilities and stick to them.

One final question is needed: Am I serving God now?

Upon reading this, you may start feeling restless. *Maybe I need to change jobs. Perhaps I should relocate. I guess Max is telling me I need to go to seminary . . .* No, not necessarily.

Again, Jesus is the ideal example. When do we get our first clue that he knows he is the Son of God? In the temple of Jerusalem. He is twelve years old. His parents are three days into the return trip to Nazareth before they notice he is missing.

They find him in the temple studying with the leaders. When they ask him for an explanation, he says, "Did you not know that I must be about My Father's business?" (Luke 2:49 NKJV).

As a young boy, Jesus already senses the call of God. But what does he do next? Recruit apostles and preach sermons and perform miracles? No, he goes home to his folks and learns the family business.

That is exactly what you should do. Want to bring focus

to your life? Do what Jesus did. Go home, love your family, and take care of business. *But Max, I want to be a missionary.* Your first mission field is under your roof. What makes you think they'll believe you overseas if they don't believe you across the hall?

But Max, I'm ready to do great things for God. Good, do them at work. Be a good employee. Show up on time with a good attitude. Don't complain or grumble, but "work as if you were doing it for the Lord, not for people" (Col. 3:23).

The P.L.A.N.

Pretty simple plan, don't you think? It's even easy to remember. Perhaps you caught the acrostic:

> Am I fitting into God's *P*lan?
> What are my *L*ongings?
> What are my *A*bilities?
> Am I serving God *N*ow?

THINKING

Answer the first and last questions with more than a yes or no. To what degree do you feel you are fitting into God's plan? In how many different ways are you serving God right now?

Make a list of your longings and then read it out loud after asking, "Are these the things that really represent my deepest heart-longings?"

Ask three people who know you in different settings to tell you what abilities they have noticed you using in those situations. This will help you answer the third question in the P.L.A.N.

HEARING
Psalm 139:14 NLT:

> Thank you for making me so wonderfully complex!
> Your workmanship is marvelous—and how well
> I know it.

REFLECTING
If the verse above seems awkward or unfamiliar, you should take time to read the first eighteen verses of Psalm 139. How often do you thank your Creator for making you "complex"?

When you speak to the Lord, how would you apply the terms *wonderful*, *workmanship*, and *marvelous* to yourself?

SPEAKING

Look back over what you have thought and written about the P.L.A.N. Turn those thoughts and feelings into a prayer of dedication to God's work in and through your life.

Restate David's thanksgiving prayer in Psalm 139, giving details to back up your gratitude to the Lord.

Behold, You desire truth in the inward parts,
And in the hidden part You will make me to know wisdom.
—Psalm 51:6 NKJV

An Honest Heart

A woman stands before judge and jury, places one hand on the Bible and the other in the air, and makes a pledge. For the next few minutes, with God as her helper, she will "tell the truth, the whole truth, and nothing but the truth."

She is a witness. Her job is neither to expand upon nor dilute the truth. Her job is to tell the truth. Leave it to the legal counsel to interpret. Leave it to the jury to resolve. Leave it to the judge to apply. But the witness? The witness speaks the truth. Let her do more or less and she taints the outcome. But let her do that—let her tell the truth—and justice has a chance.

The Christian, too, is a witness. We, too, make a pledge. Like the witness in court, we are called to tell the truth. The bench may be absent and the judge unseen, but the Bible is present, the watching world is the jury, and we are the primary witnesses. We are subpoenaed by no less than Jesus himself: "You will be my witnesses—in Jerusalem, in all of Judea, in Samaria, and in every part of the world" (Acts 1:8).

We are witnesses. And like witnesses in a court, we are called to testify, to tell what we have seen and heard. And we are to speak truthfully. Our task is neither to whitewash nor bloat the truth. Our task is to tell the truth. Period.

There is, however, one difference between the witness in court and the witness for Christ. The witness in court eventually steps down from the witness chair, but the witness for Christ never does. Since the claims of Christ are always on trial, court is perpetually in session, and we remain under oath. For the Christian, deception is never an option. It wasn't an option for Jesus.

One of the most astounding assessments of Christ is this summary: "He had done nothing wrong, and he had never lied" (Isa. 53:9). Jesus was staunchly honest. His every word accurate, his every sentence true. No cheating on tests. No altering the accounts. Not once did Jesus stretch the truth. Not once did he shade the truth. Not once did he avoid the truth. He simply told the truth. No deceit was found in his mouth.

And if God has his way with us, none will be found in ours. He longs for us to be just like Jesus. His plan, if you remember, is to shape us along the lines of his Son (Rom. 8:28). He seeks not to decrease or minimize our deception but to eliminate our deception. God is blunt about dishonesty: "No one who is dishonest will live in my house" (Ps. 101:7).

Our Master has a strict honor code. From Genesis to Revelation, the theme is the same: God loves the truth and hates deceit. In 1 Corinthians 6:9–10, Paul listed the type of people who will not inherit the kingdom of God. The covey he portrays is a ragged assortment of those who sin sexually, worship idols, take part in adultery, sell their bodies, get drunk, rob people, and—there it is—*lie about others.*

Such rigor may surprise you. *You mean my fibbing and flattering stir the same heavenly anger as adultery and aggravated assault?* Apparently so. God views fudging on income taxes the same way he views kneeling before idols.

> The LORD hates those who tell lies but is pleased with those who keep their promises. (Prov. 12:22)

> The LORD hates . . . a lying tongue. (Prov. 6:16–17)

> [God] destroy[s] liars . . . [and] hates those who kill and trick others. (Ps. 5:6)

Why? Why the hard line? Why the tough stance?

For one reason: dishonesty is absolutely contrary to the character of God. According to Hebrews 6:18, it is impossible for God to lie. It's not that God will not lie or that he has chosen not to lie—he *cannot* lie. For God to lie is for a dog to fly and a bird to bark. It simply cannot happen. The book of Titus echoes the same three words as the book of Hebrews: "God cannot lie" (Titus 1:2).

God always speaks truth. When he makes a covenant, he keeps it. When he makes a statement, he means it. And when he proclaims the truth, we can believe it. What he says is true. Even "if we are not faithful, [God] will still be faithful, because he cannot be false to himself" (2 Tim. 2:13).

Satan, on the other hand, finds it impossible to tell the truth. According to Jesus, the devil is "the father of lies" (John 8:44). If you'll remember, deceit was the first tool out of the devil's bag. In the garden of Eden, Satan didn't discourage Eve. He didn't seduce her. He didn't sneak up on her. He just lied to her. "God says you'll die if you eat the fruit? You will not die" (see Gen. 3:1–4).

Big Fat Liar. But Eve was suckered, and the fruit was plucked, and it's not more than a few paragraphs before husband and son are following suit and the honesty of Eden seems a distant memory.

It still does. Daniel Webster was right when he observed, "There is nothing as powerful as the truth and often nothing as strange."

THINKING

In what ways do you think truth brings toughness to the heart?

What do you find comforting about God's inability to lie?

In what areas of your life do you find truthfulness to be a recurring challenge and a growing edge?

HEARING

Ephesians 4:15–16 NIV:

> Instead, speaking the truth in love, we will in all things grow up into him who is the Head, that is, Christ. From him the whole body, joined and held together by every supporting ligament, grows and builds itself up in love, as each part does its work.

REFLECTING

Is "speaking the truth in love" more a description of the motivation behind speaking the truth or a description of the way in which truth is spoken?

How does truth prevent decay and foster good health in every way?

In what ways does the Scripture above make the point that there is much more at stake in speaking the truth than personal preference?

SPEAKING

Ask the Lord to help you see where dishonesty has invaded a relationship in your life and to take steps to set things right.

Thank God for his unwavering honesty with you, speaking truth to you in love as well as in discipline and correction.

When Jesus spoke again to the people, he said, "I am the light of the world. Whoever follows me will never walk in darkness, but will have the light of life."
—John 8:12 NIV

A Heart with Integrity

According to a *Psychology Today* survey, the devil is still spinning webs, and we are still plucking fruit.

▶ More people say they have cheated on their marriage partners than on their tax returns or expense accounts.

▶ More than half say that if their tax returns were audited, they would probably owe the government money.

▶ About one out of three people admits to deceiving a best friend about something within the last year; 96 percent of them feel guilty about it.

▶ Nearly half predict that if they scratched another car in the parking lot, they would drive away without leaving a note although the vast majority—89 percent—agree that would be immoral.*

---

* James Hassett, "But That Would Be Wrong," *Psychology Today*, November 1981: 34–41.

Perhaps the question shouldn't be "Why does God demand such honesty?" but rather "Why do we tolerate such dishonesty?" Never was Jeremiah more the prophet than when he announced: "The heart is deceitful above all things" (Jer. 17:9 NIV). How do we explain our dishonesty? What's the reason for our forked tongues and greasy promises? We don't need a survey to find the answer.

For one thing, we don't like the truth. Most of us can sympathize with the fellow who received a call from his wife just as she was about to fly home from Europe:

"How's my cat?" she asked.

"Dead."

"Oh, honey, don't be so honest. Why didn't you break the news to me slowly? You've ruined my trip."

"What do you mean?"

"You could have told me he was on the roof. And when I called you from Paris, you could have told me he was acting sluggish. Then when I called from London, you could have said he was sick, and when I called you from New York, you could have said he was at the vet. Then, when I arrived home, you could have said he was dead."

The husband had never been exposed to such protocol but was willing to learn. "Okay," he said. "I'll do better next time."

"By the way," she asked, "how's Mom?"

There was a long silence, then he replied, "Uh, she's on the roof."

The plain fact is that we don't like the truth. Our credo is *You shall know the truth, and the truth shall make you squirm.* Our dislike for the truth began at the age of three when Mom walked into our rooms and asked, "Did you hit your little brother?" We knew then and there that honesty had its consequences. So we learned to, uhhh, well, it's not *really* lying . . . we learned to cover things up.

"Did I hit baby brother? That all depends on how you interpret the word *hit*. I mean, sure I made contact with him, but would a jury consider it a hit? Everything is relative, you know."

"Did I hit baby brother? Yes, Dad, I did. But it's not my fault. Had I been born with nonaggressive chromosomes, and had you not permitted me to watch television, it never would have happened. So, you can say I hit my brother, but the fault isn't mine. I'm a victim of nurture and nature."

The truth, we learn early, is not fun. We don't like the truth.

Not only do we not like the truth, we don't trust the truth. If we are brutally honest (which is advisable in a discussion on honesty), we'd have to admit that the truth seems inadequate to do what we need done.

We want our bosses to like us, so we flatter. We call it polishing the apple. God calls it a lie.

We want people to admire us, so we exaggerate. We call it stretching the truth. God calls it a lie.

We want people to respect us, so we live in houses we can't afford and charge bills we can't pay. We call it the American way. God calls it living a lie.

If We Don't Tell the Truth

Ananias and Sapphira represent just how much we humans do not trust the truth. They sold a piece of property and gave half the money to the church. They lied to Peter and the apostles, claiming that the land sold for the amount they gave. Their sin was not in holding back some of the money for themselves; it was in misrepresenting the truth. Their deceit resulted in their deaths. Luke wrote: "The whole church and all the others who heard about these things were filled with fear" (Acts 5:11).

More than once I've heard people refer to this story with a nervous chuckle and say, "I'm glad God doesn't still strike people dead for lying." I'm not so sure he doesn't. It seems to me that the wages of deceit is still death. Not death of the body, perhaps, but the death of:

- *a marriage*—Falsehoods are termites in the trunk of the family tree.
- *a conscience*—The tragedy of the second lie is that it is always easier to tell than the first.
- *a career*—Just ask the student who got booted out for cheating or the employee who got fired for embezzlement if the lie wasn't fatal.
- *faith*—The language of faith and the language of falsehood have two different vocabularies. Those fluent in the language of falsehood find terms like *confession* and *repentance* hard to pronounce.

We could also list the deaths of intimacy, trust, peace, credibility, and self-respect. But perhaps the most tragic death that occurs from deceit is our witness. The court won't listen to the testimony of a perjured witness. Neither will the world. Do we think our coworkers will believe our words about Christ when they can't even believe our words about how we handled our expense account? Even more significantly, do we think God will use us as witnesses if we won't tell the truth?

Every high school football team has a player whose

assignment is to carry the play from the coach to the huddle. What if the player doesn't tell the truth? What if the coach calls for a pass but the courier says the coach called for a run? One thing is certain: the coach won't call on that player very long. God says if we are faithful with the small things, he'll trust us with the greater things (Matt. 25:21). Can he trust you with the small things?

THINKING

How did you identify with the list of things that experience death as a result of dishonesty?

Think of an illustration from your own life in which the failure to be honest had devastating consequences in other areas.

What "little thing" between you and God has been giving you the greatest challenge in the area of faithfulness?

HEARING

2 Timothy 2:11–13 NIV:

Here is a trustworthy saying:

If we died with him,
　　we will also live with him;
if we endure,
　　we will also reign with him.
If we disown him,
　　he will also disown us;
if we are faithless,
　　he will remain faithful,
　　　　for he cannot disown himself.

REFLECTING

What does Paul mean by "if we died with him" as a basis for claiming that we will "live with him," meaning Christ Jesus?

Notice the last two "if" statements. How are they different? Why does "disowning" receive "disowning" in return, but faithlessness receive faithfulness in response?

In what ways do you find Paul's last statement there both deeply honest and comforting at the same time: "if we are faithless, he will remain faithful, for he cannot disown himself"?

SPEAKING

If you're feeling unmasked and vulnerable with all this talk about honesty, you may need to talk to God about some serious heart scrubbing. A good way to start is by telling God you don't even know where to start.

Let the phrase, "when I am faithless you remain faithful" sink into your soul for a few moments, and then express your gratitude to God for his unwavering faithfulness.

Above all else, guard your heart,
for it is the wellspring of life.
—Proverbs 4:23 NIV

A Guarded Heart

You've got to admit some of our hearts are trashed out. Let any riffraff knock on the door, and we throw it open. Anger shows up, and we let him in. Revenge needs a place to stay, so we have him pull up a chair. Pity wants to have a party, so we show him the kitchen. Lust rings the bell, and we change the sheets on the bed. Don't we know how to say no?

Many don't. For most of us, thought management is, well, unthought of. We think much about time management, weight management, personnel management, even scalp management. But what about thought management? Shouldn't we be as concerned about managing our thoughts as we are managing anything else? Jesus was. Like a trained soldier at the gate of a city, he stood watch over his mind. He stubbornly guarded the gateway of his heart. Many thoughts were denied entrance. Need a few examples?

How about arrogance? On one occasion the people determined to make Jesus their king. What an attractive thought. Most of us would delight in the notion of royalty. Even if we refused the crown, we would enjoy considering the invitation. Not Jesus. "Jesus saw that in their enthusiasm, they were about to grab him and make him king, so he slipped off and went back up the mountain to be by himself" (John 6:15 MSG).

Another dramatic example occurred in a conversation Jesus had with Peter. Upon hearing Jesus announce his impending death on the cross, the impetuous apostle objected. "Impossible, Master! That can never be!" (Matt. 16:22 MSG). Apparently, Peter was about to question the necessity of Calvary. But he never had a chance. Christ blocked the doorway. He sent both the messenger and the author of the heresy scurrying: "Peter, get out of my way. Satan, get lost. You have no idea how God works" (v. 23 MSG).

And how about the time Jesus was mocked? Have you ever had people laugh at you? Jesus did too. Responding to an appeal to heal a sick girl, he entered her house only to be told she was dead. His response? "The child is not dead but sleeping." The response of the people in the house? "They laughed at him." Just like all of us, Jesus had to face a moment of humiliation. But unlike most of us, he refused to receive it. Note his decisive response: "he put them all outside" (Mark 5:39, 40 RSV). The mockery was allowed neither in the house of the girl nor in the mind of Christ.

Jesus guarded his heart. If he did, shouldn't we do the same? Most certainly! "Be careful what you think, because your thoughts run your life" (Prov. 4:23). Jesus wants your heart to be fertile and fruitful. He wants you to have a heart like his. That is God's goal for you. He wants you to "think and act like Christ Jesus" (Phil. 2:5). But how? The answer is surprisingly simple. We can be transformed if we make one decision: *I will submit my thoughts to the authority of Jesus.*

It's easy to overlook a significant claim made by Christ at the conclusion of Matthew's gospel. "All authority in heaven and on earth has been given to me" (Matt. 28:18 NIV). Jesus claims to be the CEO of heaven and earth. He has the ultimate say on everything, especially our thoughts. He has more authority, for example, than your parents. Your parents may say you are no good, but Jesus says you are valuable, and he has authority over parents. He even has more authority over you than you do. You may tell yourself that you are too bad to be forgiven, but Jesus has a different opinion. If you give him authority over you, then your guilty thoughts are no longer allowed.

Jesus also has authority over your ideas. Suppose you have an idea that you want to rob a grocery store. Jesus, however, has made it clear that stealing is wrong. If you have given him authority over your ideas, then the idea of stealing cannot remain in your thoughts.

See what I mean by authority? To have a pure heart, we must submit all thoughts to the authority of Christ. If we are willing to do that, he will change us to be like him.

Tomorrow, we will see how it works.

THINKING

Personalize the statement from the devotional: "To have a pure heart, I must submit all thoughts to the authority of Christ."

What feels good about submission to Christ?

How does thought management go together with heart management?

HEARING

Matthew 12:33–35 NLT:

> "A tree is identified by its fruit. Make a tree good, and its fruit will be good. Make a tree bad, and its fruit will be bad. You brood of snakes! How could evil men like you speak what is good and right? For whatever is in your heart determines what you say. A good person produces good words from a good heart, and an evil person produces evil words from an evil heart."

REFLECTING

Identify the items Jesus mentioned: tree, fruit, and those involved in making a tree bad or good.

As you review your statements over the last twenty-four-hour period, what would you say the quality of your words indicates about the condition of your heart?

Have you ever made the deliberate, conscious decision to "submit your thoughts to the authority of Jesus"? What difference has that decision made in your life?

SPEAKING

If you never have made the decision to formally, audibly submit to the authority of Jesus Christ, is there anything that would keep you from doing that right now?

Thank God for the consistent, powerful example of a guarded heart that Jesus left for us to follow.

*And so, dear brothers and sisters who belong to God
and are bound for heaven, think about this Jesus whom
we declare to be God's Messenger and High Priest.*
—Hebrews 3:1 NLT

Posting a Guard

Your heart is a fertile greenhouse ready to produce good fruit. Your mind is the doorway to your heart—the strategic place where you determine which seeds are sown and which seeds are discarded. The Holy Spirit is ready to help you manage and filter the thoughts that try to enter. He can help you guard your heart.

He stands with you on the threshold. A thought approaches, a questionable thought. Do you throw open the door and let it enter? Of course not. You "fight to capture every thought until it acknowledges the authority of Christ" (2 Cor. 10:5 PHILLIPS). You don't leave the door unguarded. You stand equipped with handcuffs and leg irons, ready to capture any thought not fit to enter.

For the sake of discussion, let's say a thought regarding your personal value approaches. With all the cockiness of a neighborhood bully, the thought swaggers up to the door and says, "You're a loser. All your life you've been a loser. You've blown relationships and jobs and ambitions. You might as well write the word *bum* on your résumé, for that is what you are."

The ordinary person would throw open the door and let the thought in. Like a seed from a weed, it would find fertile soil and take root and bear thorns of inferiority. The average person would say, "You're right. I'm a bum. Come on in."

But as a Christian, you aren't your average person. You are led by the Spirit. So rather than let the thought in, you take it captive. You handcuff it and march it down the street to the courthouse where you present the thought before the judgment seat of Christ.

"Jesus, this thought says I'm a bum and a loser and that I'll never amount to anything. What do you think?"

See what you are doing? You are submitting the thought to the authority of Jesus. If Jesus agrees with the thought, then let it in. If not, kick it out. In this case Jesus disagrees.

How do you know if Jesus agrees or disagrees? You open your Bible. What does God think about you? Ephesians 2:10 is a good place to check: "For we are God's workmanship, created in Christ Jesus to do good works, which God prepared in advance for us to do" (NIV). Or how about Romans 8:1: "There is now no condemnation for those who are in Christ Jesus" (NIV)?

Obviously any thought that says you are inferior or insignificant does not pass the test—and does not gain entrance. You have the right to give the bully a firm kick in the pants and watch him run.

Let's take another example. The first thought was a bully; this next thought is a groupie. She comes not to tell you how bad you are but how good you are. She rushes to the doorway and gushes, "You are so good. You are so wonderful. The world is so lucky to have you," and on and on the groupie grovels.

Typically this is the type of thought you'd welcome. But

you don't do things the typical way. You guard your heart. You walk in the Spirit. And you take every thought captive. So once again you go to Jesus. You submit this thought to the authority of Christ. As you unsheathe the sword of the Spirit, his Word, you learn that pride doesn't please God.

> Don't cherish exaggerated ideas of yourself or your importance. (Rom. 12:3 PHILLIPS)

> The cross of our Lord Jesus Christ is my only reason for bragging. (Gal. 6:14)

As much as you'd like to welcome this thought of conceit into the greenhouse, you can't. You only allow what Christ allows.

One more example. This time the thought is not one of criticism or flattery, but one of temptation. If you're a fellow, the thought is dressed in flashy red. If you're a female, the thought is the hunk you've always wanted. There is the brush of the hand, the fragrance in the air, and the invitation. "Come on, it's all right. We're consenting adults."

What do you do? Well, if you aren't under the authority of Christ, you throw open the door. But if you have the mind of Christ, you step back and say, "Not so fast. You'll have to get permission from my big brother." So you take this steamy act before Jesus and ask, "Yes or no?"

Nowhere does he answer more clearly than in 1 Corinthians 6 and 7: "We must not pursue the kind of sex that avoids commitment and intimacy, leaving us more lonely than ever. . . . Is it a good thing to have sexual relations? Certainly—but only within a certain context. It's good for a man to have a wife, and for a woman to have a husband. Sexual drives are strong, but marriage is strong enough to contain them" (6:18; 7:1, 2 MSG).

Now armed with the opinion of Christ and the sword of the Spirit, what do you do? Well, if the tempter is not your spouse, close the door. If the invitation is from your spouse, then *hubba, hubba, hubba.*

The point is this. Guard the doorway of your heart. Submit your thoughts to the authority of Christ. The more selective you are about seeds, the more delighted you will be with the crop.

THINKING

What's the password to your heart and who knows it?

In what kinds of situations does your heart feel most vulnerable and poorly guarded?

What did you find most helpful about the examples of specific ways to capture and submit thoughts to the authority of Jesus Christ?

HEARING

Philippians 4:4–10 NIV:

> Rejoice in the Lord always. I will say it again:
> Rejoice! Let your gentleness be evident to all. The
> Lord is near. Do not be anxious about anything, but
> in everything, by prayer and petition, with thanks-
> giving, present your requests to God. And the peace
> of God, which transcends all understanding, will
> guard your hearts and your minds in Christ Jesus.
> Finally, brothers, whatever is true, whatever is noble,
> whatever is right, whatever is pure, whatever is lovely,
> whatever is admirable—if anything is excellent or
> praiseworthy—think about such things. Whatever
> you have learned or received or heard from me, or
> seen in me—put it into practice. And the God of
> peace will be with you.

REFLECTING

What specific actions does this passage tell us will lead to
our hearts and minds being guarded?

How many good seeds for thought can you identify in this
passage?

Paul mentions "peace" twice. What does peace have to do with a guarded heart?

SPEAKING

Use the following list as a framework for a conversation with God. Thank him for all the examples in your life that represent each of these traits: things that are true, noble, right, pure, lovely, admirable—anything excellent or praiseworthy.

Commit yourself in prayer to practice the discipline of taking suspicious thoughts captive and submitting them to the authority of Jesus.

*Your eyes are windows into your body. If you open your eyes wide
in wonder and belief, your body fills up with light. If you live
squinty-eyed in greed and distrust, your body is a dank cellar.*
—Matthew 6:22–23 MSG

The Hope-Filled Heart

On the night before his death, a veritable landfill of
woes tumbled in on Jesus. Somewhere between the
Gethsemane prayer and the mock trial is what has to
be the darkest scene in the history of the human drama.
Though the entire episode couldn't have totaled more than
five minutes, the event had enough badness to fill a thousand
Dumpsters. Except for Christ, not one person did one good
thing. Search the scene for an ounce of courage or a speck of
character, and you won't find it. What you will find is a com-
post heap of deceit and betrayal. Yet in it all, Jesus saw reason
to hope. And in his outlook, we find an example to follow.

> "Get up, we must go. Look, here comes the man who
> has turned against me."
> While Jesus was still speaking, Judas, one of
> the twelve apostles, came up. With him were many
> people carrying swords and clubs who had been sent
> from the leading priests and the older Jewish lead-
> ers of the people. Judas had planned to give them a

signal, saying, "The man I kiss is Jesus. Arrest him." At once Judas went to Jesus and said, "Greetings, Teacher!" and kissed him.

Jesus answered, "Friend, do what you came to do."

Then the people came and grabbed Jesus and arrested him. When that happened, one of Jesus' followers reached for his sword and pulled it out. He struck the servant of the high priest and cut off his ear.

Jesus said to the man, "Put your sword back in its place. All who use swords will be killed with swords. Surely you know I could ask my Father, and he would give me more than twelve armies of angels. But it must happen this way to bring about what the Scriptures say."

Then Jesus said to the crowd, "You came to get me with swords and clubs as if I were a criminal. Every day I sat in the Temple teaching, and you did not arrest me there. But all these things have happened so that it will come about as the prophets wrote." Then all of Jesus' followers left him and ran away. (Matt. 26:46–56)

Had a reporter been assigned to cover the arrest, his headline might have read:

A DARK NIGHT FOR JESUS
Galilean preacher abandoned by friends

Last Friday they welcomed him with palm leaves. Last night they arrested him with swords. The world of Jesus of Nazareth turned sour as he was apprehended by a crowd of soldiers and angry citizens in a garden just outside the city walls. Only a week since his triumphant entry, his popularity has taken a fatal plunge. Even his followers refuse to claim him. The disciples who took pride in being seen with him earlier in the week took flight from him last night. With the public crying for his death and the disciples denying any involvement, the future of this celebrated teacher appears bleak, and the impact of his mission appears limited.

The darkest night of Jesus' life was marked by one crisis after another. In just a moment we will see what Jesus saw, but first let's consider what an observer would have witnessed in the Garden of Gethsemane.

First he would have seen *unanswered prayer*. Jesus had just offered an anguished appeal to God. "My Father, if it is possible, do not give me this cup of suffering. But do what you want, not what I want" (Matt. 26:39). This was no calm, serene hour of prayer. Matthew says that Jesus was "very sad and troubled" (v. 37). The Master "fell to the ground" (v. 39) and cried out to God. Luke tells us that Jesus was "full of pain" and that "his sweat was like drops of blood falling to the ground" (Luke 22:44).

Never has earth offered such an urgent request. And never has heaven offered more deafening silence. The prayer of Jesus was unanswered. *Jesus* and *unanswered prayer* in the same phrase? Isn't that an oxymoron? Would the son of Henry have no Ford or the child of Bill Gates own no computer? Would God, the one who owns the cattle on a thousand hills, keep something from his own Son? He did that night. Consequently,

Jesus had to deal with the dilemma of unanswered prayer. And that was just the beginning. Look who showed up next:

> With [Judas] were many people carrying swords and clubs who had been sent from the leading priests and the older Jewish leaders of the people. . . . Then the people came and grabbed Jesus and arrested him. (Matt. 26:47, 50)

Judas arrived with an angry crowd. Again, from the perspective of an observer, this crowd represents another crisis. Not only did Jesus have to face unanswered prayer, he also had to deal with *unfruitful service*. The very people he came to save had now come to arrest him.

Let me give you a fact that may alter your impression of that night. Perhaps you envision Judas leading a dozen or so soldiers who are carrying two or three lanterns. Matthew wrote, however, that "many people" came to arrest Jesus. John was even more specific. The term he employed is the Greek word *speira*, or a "group of soldiers" (John 18:3). At minimum, *speira* depicts a group of two hundred soldiers. It can describe a detachment as large as nineteen hundred!*

Equipped with John's description, we'd be more accurate to imagine a river of several hundred troops entering the garden. Add to that figure untold watchers whom Matthew simply calls "the crowd," and you have a mob of people.

Surely in a group this size there is one person who will defend Jesus. He came to the aid of so many. All those sermons.

---

* William Barclay, *The Gospel of John*, vol. 2 (Philadelphia: The Westminster Press, 1975), 222.

All those miracles. Now they will bear fruit. And so we wait for the one person who will declare, "Jesus is an innocent man!" But no one does. Not one person speaks out on his behalf. The people he came to save have turned against him.

We can almost forgive the crowd. Their contact with Jesus was too brief, too casual. Perhaps they didn't know better. But the disciples did. They knew better. They knew *him* better. But do they defend Jesus? Hardly. The most bitter pill Jesus had to swallow was the *unbelievable betrayal* by the disciples.

Judas wasn't the only turncoat. Matthew was admirably honest when he confessed, "All of Jesus' followers left him and ran away" (26:56).

For such a short word, *all* sure packs some pain. "*All* of Jesus' followers . . . ran away." John did. Matthew did. Simon did. Thomas did. They all did. We don't have to go far to find the last time this word was used. Note the verse just a few lines before our text: "But Peter said, 'I will never say that I don't know you! I will even die with you!' And *all* the other followers said the same thing" (v. 35, emphasis mine).

All pledged loyalty, and yet *all* ran. From the outside looking in, all we see is betrayal. The disciples have left him. The people have rejected him. And God hasn't heard him. Never has so much trash been dumped on one being. Stack all the disloyalties of deadbeat dads and cheating wives and prodigal kids and dishonest workers in one pile, and you begin to see what Jesus had to face that night. From a human point of view, Jesus' world has collapsed. No answer from heaven, no help from the people, no loyalty from his friends.

Jesus, neck-deep in rubbish. That's how I would have described the scene. That's how a reporter would have described it. That's how a witness would have portrayed it. But that's not how Jesus saw it. He saw something else entirely. He wasn't oblivious to the trash; he just wasn't limited to it. Somehow he was able to see good in the bad, the purpose in the pain, and God's presence in the problem.

We could use a little of Jesus' 20/20 vision, couldn't we? You and I live in a trashy world. Unwanted garbage comes our way on a regular basis. We, too, have unanswered prayers and unfruitful dreams and unbelievable betrayals, do we not? Haven't you been handed a trash sack of mishaps and heart-aches? Sure you have. May I ask, what are you going to do with it?

THINKING

Which of these unwanted garbage piles do you have the hardest time looking past: unanswered prayers, unfruitful dreams, or unbelievable betrayals?

What answer echoed in your heart when you read the closing question about the trash you've been handed: "What are you going to do with it?"

Describe what you understand to be the experience of a hope-filled heart.

HEARING

Romans 5:3–5 NIV:

> Not only so, but we also rejoice in our sufferings,
> because we know that suffering produces persever-
> ance; perseverance, character; and character, hope.
> And hope does not disappoint us, because God has
> poured out his love into our hearts by the Holy
> Spirit, whom he has given us.

REFLECTING

What steps does Paul indicate will be required in order to
develop a genuinely hope-filled heart?

What seems to be the relationship between hope and love in
the way this passage connects the two?

How large a challenge is it for you to be able to rejoice in
your sufferings? In what present situations can you practice
that attitude?

SPEAKING

Prayerfully consider having a conversation with one or two older Christians who have demonstrated an attitude of hope. Tell them you want to have a 1 Peter 3:15 conversation.

Ask the Lord to remind you in moments of discomfort and suffering to begin the hope process by rejoicing.

*God did this so that, by two unchangeable things in which
it is impossible for God to lie, we who have fled to take hold
of the hope offered to us may be greatly encouraged. We
have this hope as an anchor for the soul, firm and secure.
It enters the inner sanctuary behind the curtain, where
Jesus, who went before us, has entered on our behalf.*
—Hebrews 6:18–20 NIV

Learning Hope
from the Master

You have several options when life seems to hand you a
pile of garbage. You could hide it. You could take the
trash bag and cram it under your coat or stick it under your
dress and pretend it isn't there. But you and I know you won't
fool anyone. Besides, sooner or later it will start to stink. Or
you could disguise it. Paint it green, put it on the front lawn,
and tell everybody it is a tree. Again, no one will be fooled,
and pretty soon it's going to reek. So what will you do? If
you follow the example of Christ, you will learn to see tough
times differently. Remember, God loves you just the way you
are, but he refuses to leave you that way. He wants you to
have a hope-filled heart . . . just like Jesus.

Here is what Christ did.

He found good in the bad. It would be hard to find

someone worse than Judas. Some say he was a good man with a backfired strategy. I don't buy that. The Bible says, "Judas . . . was a thief. He was the one who kept the money box, and he often stole from it" (John 12:6). The man was a crook. Somehow he was able to live in the presence of God and experience the miracles of Christ and remain unchanged. In the end he decided he'd rather have money than a friend, so he sold Jesus for thirty pieces of silver. I'm sorry, but every human life is worth more than thirty pieces of silver. Judas was a scoundrel, a cheat, and a bum. How could anyone see him any other way?

I don't know, but Jesus did. Only inches from the face of his betrayer, Jesus looked at him and said, "Friend, do what you came to do" (Matt. 26:50). What Jesus saw in Judas as worthy of being called a friend, I can't imagine. But I do know that Jesus doesn't lie, and in that moment he saw something good in a very bad man.

It would help if we did the same. How can we? Again Jesus gives us guidance. He didn't place all the blame on Judas. He saw another presence that night: "this is . . . the time when darkness rules" (Luke 22:53). In no way was Judas innocent, but neither was Judas acting alone. Your attackers aren't acting alone either. "Our fight is not against people on earth but against the rulers and authorities and the powers of this world's darkness, against the spiritual powers of evil in the heavenly world" (Eph. 6:12).

Those who betray us are victims of a fallen world. We needn't place all the blame on them. Jesus found enough good in the face of Judas to call him friend, and he can help us do the same with those who hurt us.

Not only did Jesus find good in the bad, *he found purpose*

in the pain. Of the ninety-eight words Jesus spoke at his arrest, thirty refer to the purpose of God.

> "It must happen this way to bring about what the Scriptures say." (Matt. 26:54)

> "All these things have happened so that it will come about as the prophets wrote." (v. 56)

Jesus chose to see his immediate struggle as a necessary part of a greater plan. He viewed the Gethsemane conflict as an important but singular act in the grand manuscript of God's drama.

I witnessed something similar on a recent trip. My daughter Andrea and I were flying to St. Louis. Because of storms, the flight was delayed and then diverted to another city where we sat on the runway waiting for the rain clouds to pass. As I was glancing at my watch and drumming my fingers, wondering when we would arrive, the fellow across the aisle tapped me on the arm and asked if he could borrow my Bible. I handed it to him. He turned to a young girl in the adjacent seat, opened the Bible, and read the Scriptures with her for the remainder of the trip.

After some time, the sky cleared, and we resumed our journey. We were landing in St. Louis when he returned the Bible to me and explained in a low voice that this was the girl's first flight. She recently had joined the military and was leaving home for the first time. He asked her if she believed in Christ, and she said she wanted to but didn't know how. That's when he borrowed my Bible and told her about Jesus. By the time we landed, she told him she believed in Jesus as the Son of God.

I've since wondered about that event. Did God bring the storm so the girl could hear the gospel? Did God delay our arrival so she'd have ample time to learn about Jesus? I wouldn't put it past him. That is how Jesus chose to view the storm that came his way: necessary turbulence in the plan of God. Where others saw gray skies, Jesus saw a divine order. His suffering was necessary to fulfill prophecy, and his sacrifice was necessary to fulfill the law.

Wouldn't you love to have a hope-filled heart? Wouldn't you love to see the world through the eyes of Jesus? Where we see unanswered prayer, Jesus saw answered prayer. Where we see the absence of God, Jesus saw the plan of God. Note especially Matthew 26:53: "Surely you know I could ask my Father, and he would give me more than twelve armies of angels." Of all the treasures Jesus saw in the trash, this is most significant. *He saw his Father.* He saw his Father's presence in the problem. Twelve armies of angels were within his sight.

Sure, Max, but Jesus was God. He could see the unseen. He had eyes for heaven and a vision for the supernatural. I can't see the way he saw.

Not yet maybe, but don't underestimate God's power. He can change the way you look at life.

Need proof? How about the example of Elisha and his servant? The two were in Dothan when an angry king sent his army to destroy them.

> Elisha's servant got up early, and when he went out, he saw an army with horses and chariots all around the city. The servant said to Elisha, "Oh, my master, what can we do?"

Elisha said, "Don't be afraid. The army that fights for us is larger than the one against us."

Then Elisha prayed, "LORD, open my servant's eyes, and let him see."

The LORD opened the eyes of the young man, and he saw that the mountain was full of horses and chariots of fire all around Elisha. (2 Kings 6:15–17)

By God's power, the servant saw the angels. Who is to say the same can't happen for you?

God never promises to remove us from our struggles. He does promise, however, to change the way we look at them. The apostle Paul dedicated a paragraph to listing trash bags: troubles, problems, sufferings, hunger, nakedness, danger, and violent death (Rom. 8:35). These are the very Dumpsters of difficulty we hope to escape. Paul, however, stated their value: "In all these things we are completely victorious through God" (v. 37). We'd prefer other prepositions. We'd opt for "*apart from* all these things," "*away from* all these things," or even "*without* all these things." But Paul said, "*in* all these things." The solution is not to avoid trouble but to change the way we see our troubles.

God can correct your vision.

He asks, "Who gives a person sight?" then answers, "It is I, the LORD" (Ex. 4:11). God let Balaam see the angel, Elisha see the army, Jacob see the ladder, and Saul see the Savior. More than one have made the request of the blind man, "Teacher, I want to see" (Mark 10:51). And more than one have walked away with clear vision. Who is to say God won't do the same for you?

THINKING

How do you feel about the garbage that has come your way so far in life?

Which would you say has been your heart's tendency: to allow the garbage to influence your view of God or to allow your relationship with God to influence your view of the garbage?

Jesus saw good in the bad, purpose in the pain, and his Father in all things. Which of these three "lenses" would create the biggest change in your heart's perspective?

HEARING

Romans 12:9–16 NKJV:

> Let love be without hypocrisy. Abhor what is evil. Cling to what is good. Be kindly affectionate to one another with brotherly love, in honor giving preference to one another; not lagging in diligence, fervent in spirit, serving the Lord; rejoicing in hope, patient in tribulation, continuing steadfastly in prayer; distributing to the needs of the saints, given to hospitality. Bless those who persecute you; bless and do not curse. Rejoice with those who rejoice, and weep

with those who weep. Be of the same mind toward one another. Do not set your mind on high things, but associate with the humble. Do not be wise in your own opinion.

REFLECTING

Tucked into the middle of the passage above we find a statement about hope. How does "rejoicing in hope" fit in the list of responses to life's challenges that Paul urges us to practice?

How do you think the presence of hope in your heart would affect your ability to live out each of the twenty or so brief commands listed in the passage above?

Twice in today's reading Max used the question, "Who is to say God won't do the same for you?" How did you answer the question?

SPEAKING

Make it a point to ask God to correct your vision. Humbly tell him in what ways you would like to "see" like Jesus.

Turn Romans 12:9–16 into a prayer, considering the level of hope in your heart about each of the commands, then asking God for help in improving your hope-sight in those areas.

Rejoice in the Lord always. Again I will say, rejoice!
—Philippians 4:4 NKJV

A Rejoicing Heart

y family did something thoughtful for me last night. They had a party in my honor—a surprise birthday party. Early last week I told Denalyn not to plan anything except a nice family evening at a restaurant. She listened only to the restaurant part. I was unaware that half a dozen families were going to join us.

In fact, I tried to talk her into staying at home. "Let's have the dinner on another night," I volunteered. Andrea had been sick. Jenna had homework, and I'd spent the afternoon watching football games and felt lazy—not really in a mood to get up and clean up and go out. I thought I'd have no problem convincing the girls to postpone the dinner. Boy, was I surprised! They wouldn't think of it. Each of my objections was met with a united front and a unanimous defense. My family made it clear—we were going out to eat.

Not only that, we were leaving on time. I consented and set about getting ready. But to their dismay, I moved too slowly. We were a study in contrasts. My attitude was, *Why hurry?* My daughters' attitude was, *Hurry up!* I was ho-hum. They were gung-ho. I was content to stay. They were anxious to leave. To be honest, I was bewildered by their actions. They were being uncharacteristically prompt. Curiously enthused. Why the big deal? I mean, I enjoy a night out as much as the next guy, but Sara giggled all the way to the restaurant.

Only when we arrived did their actions make sense. One step inside the door and I understood their enthusiasm. *Surprise!* No wonder they were acting differently. They knew what I didn't. They had seen what I hadn't. They'd already seen the table and stacked the gifts and smelled the cake. Since they knew about the party, they did everything necessary to see that I didn't miss it.

Jesus does the same for us. He knows about *the party*. In one of the greatest chapters in the Bible, Luke 15, he told three stories. Each story speaks of something lost and of something found. A lost sheep. A lost coin. And a lost son. And at the end of each one, Jesus described a party, a celebration. The shepherd throws the party for the lost-now-found sheep. The housewife throws a party because of the lost-now-found coin. And the father throws a party in honor of his lost-now-found son.

Three parables, each with a party. Three stories, each with the appearance of the same word: *happy*. Regarding the shepherd who found the lost sheep, Jesus said: "And when he finds it, he *happily* puts it on his shoulders and goes home" (vv. 5–6, emphasis mine). When the housewife finds her lost coin, she announces, "Be *happy* with me because I have found the coin that I lost" (v. 9, emphasis mine). And the father of the prodigal son explains to the reluctant older brother, "We had to celebrate and be *happy* because your brother was dead, but now he is alive. He was lost, but now he is found" (v. 32, emphasis mine).

The point is clear. Jesus is happiest when the lost are

found. For him, no moment compares to the moment of salvation. For my daughter the rejoicing began when I got dressed and in the car and on the road to the party. The same occurs in heaven. Let one child consent to be dressed in righteousness and begin the journey home and heaven pours the punch, strings the streamers, and throws the confetti. "There is joy in the presence of the angels of God when one sinner changes his heart and life" (v. 10).

A century ago this verse caused Charles Spurgeon to write:

> There are Christmas days in heaven where Christ's high mass is kept, and Christ is not glorified because he was born in a manger but because he is born in a broken heart. And these are days when the shepherd brings home the lost sheep upon his shoulders, when the church has swept her house and found the lost piece of money, for then are these friends and neighbors called together, and they rejoice with joy unspeakable and full of glory over one sinner who repents.*

How do we explain such joy? Why such a stir? You've got to admit, the excitement is a bit curious. We aren't talking about a nation of people or even a city of souls; we're talking about joy "when *one* sinner changes his heart and life." How could one person create that much excitement?

Who would imagine that our actions have such an impact on heaven? We can live and die and leave no more than an

* Charles Spurgeon's sermon entitled "The Sympathy of Two Worlds," quoted in John MacArthur, *The Glory of Heaven* (Wheaton, IL: Crossway Books, 1996), 246.

obituary. Our greatest actions on earth go largely unnoticed and unrecorded. Dare we think that God is paying attention?

According to this verse, he is. According to Jesus, our decisions have a thermostatic impact on the unseen world. Our actions on the keyboard of earth trigger hammers on the piano strings of heaven. Our obedience pulls the ropes that ring the bells in heaven's belfries. Let a child call, and the ear of the Father inclines. Let a sister weep, and tears begin to flow from above. Let a saint die, and the gate is opened. And most important, let a sinner repent, and every other activity ceases, and every heavenly being celebrates.

Remarkable, this response to our conversion. Heaven throws no party over our other achievements. When we graduate from school or open our business or have a baby, as far as we know, the celestial bubbly stays in the refrigerator. Why the big deal over conversion?

We don't always share such enthusiasm, do we? When you hear of a soul saved, do you drop everything and celebrate? Is your good day made better or your bad day salvaged? We may be pleased—but exuberant? Do our chests burst with joy? Do we feel an urge to call out the band and cut the cake and have a party? When a soul is saved, the heart of Jesus becomes the night sky on the Fourth of July, radiant with explosions of cheer.

Can the same be said about us? Perhaps this is one area where our hearts could use some attention.

THINKING

What does your heart do when you hear that a "sheep has been found," "the coin has been recovered," or "a wayward son has returned"?

Try to picture the reaction in heaven the day you responded to the gospel invitation?

Why do you think we tend to act and feel more like the older brother in the third parable, particularly when we have been Christians for a long time and hear about a "notorious convert," or someone who has been putting off God for years, in the closing days of life has the audacity to call out to God for mercy?

HEARING

Luke 7:40–50 NIV:

> Jesus answered him, "Simon, I have something to tell you."
>
> "Tell me, teacher," he said.
>
> "Two men owed money to a certain moneylender. One owed him five hundred denarii, and the other fifty. Neither of them had the money to pay him back,

so he canceled the debts of both. Now which of them will love him more?"

Simon replied, "I suppose the one who had the bigger debt canceled."

"You have judged correctly," Jesus said.

Then he turned toward the woman and said to Simon, "Do you see this woman? I came into your house. You did not give me any water for my feet, but she wet my feet with her tears and wiped them with her hair. You did not give me a kiss, but this woman, from the time I entered, has not stopped kissing my feet. You did not put oil on my head, but she has poured perfume on my feet. Therefore, I tell you, her many sins have been forgiven—for she loved much. But he who has been forgiven little loves little."

Then Jesus said to her, "Your sins are forgiven."

The other guests began to say among themselves, "Who is this who even forgives sins?"

Jesus said to the woman, "Your faith has saved you; go in peace."

REFLECTING

When we fail to celebrate the spiritual milestones of other people, what are we declaring about our appreciation for what God has done for us and them?

What good things can we learn and experience from the joy new Christians exude?

In what different ways have you chosen to show your deep gratitude to God for his forgiveness and grace?

SPEAKING

Make a list of people you know or have heard about who have recently made a commitment for Christ. Spend some time rejoicing with the angels, for those names are now written in the book of life.

Now try to put into words how you feel about the fact that heaven broke out in a party when you believed.

Now we see things imperfectly as in a poor mirror, but
then we will see everything with perfect clarity. All that I
know now is partial and incomplete, but then I will know
everything completely, just as God knows me now.
—1 Corinthians 13:12 NLT

The Forward-Looking Heart

*W*hy do Jesus and his angels rejoice over one repenting sinner? Can they see something we can't? Do they know something we don't? Absolutely. They know what heaven holds. They've seen the table, and they've heard the music, and they can't wait to see your face when you arrive. Better still, they can't wait to see you.

When you arrive and enter the party, something wonderful will happen. A final transformation will occur. You will be just like Jesus. Drink deeply from 1 John 3:2: "We have not yet been shown what we will be in the future. But we know that when Christ comes again, *we* will be like him" (emphasis mine).

Of all the blessings of heaven, one of the greatest will be you! You will be God's magnum opus, his work of art. The angels will gasp. God's work will be completed. At last, you will have a heart like his.

You will love with a perfect love.

You will worship with a radiant face.

You'll hear each word God speaks.

Your heart will be pure; your words will be like jewels; your thoughts will be like treasures.

You will be just like Jesus. You will, at long last, have a heart like his. Envision the heart of Jesus and you'll be envisioning your own. Guiltless. Fearless. Thrilled and joyous. Tirelessly worshiping. Flawlessly discerning. As the mountain stream is pristine and endless, so will be your heart. *You will be like him.*

And if that were not enough, everyone else will be like him as well.

"Heaven is the perfect place for people made perfect."*

Heaven is populated by those who let God change them. Arguments will cease, for jealousy won't exist. Suspicions won't surface, for there will be no secrets. Every sin is gone. Every insecurity is forgotten. Every fear is past. Pure wheat. No weeds. Pure gold. No alloy. Pure love. No lust. Pure hope. No fear. No wonder the angels rejoice when one sinner repents; they know another work of art will soon grace the gallery of God. They know what heaven holds.

There is yet another reason for the celebration. Part of the excitement is from our arrival. The other part is from our deliverance. Jesus rejoices that we are headed to heaven, but he equally rejoices that we are saved from hell.

---

* Charles Spurgeon's sermon entitled "The Sympathy of Two Worlds," quoted in John MacArthur, *The Glory of Heaven* (Wheaton, IL: Crossway Books, 1996), 118.

What We're Saved From

One phrase summarizes the horror of hell: "God isn't there."

Think for a moment about this question: What if God weren't here on earth? You think people can be cruel now; imagine us without the presence of God. You think we are brutal to each other now; imagine the world without the Holy Spirit. You think there is loneliness and despair and guilt now; imagine life without the touch of Jesus. No forgiveness. No hope. No acts of kindness. No words of love. No more food given in his name. No more songs sung to his praise. No more deeds done in his honor. If God took away his angels, his grace, his promise of eternity, and his servants, what would the world be like?

In a word, *hell*. No one to comfort you and no music to soothe you. A world where poets don't write of love and minstrels don't sing of hope, for love and hope were passengers on the last ship. The final vessel has departed, and the anthem of hell has only two words: *if only*.

According to Jesus, hell knows only the sounds of "weeping and gnashing of teeth" (Matt. 22:13 NIV). From hell comes a woeful, unending moan as its inhabitants realize the opportunity they have missed. What they would give for one more chance. But that chance is gone (Heb. 9:27).

THINKING

How does sharpening your understanding about hell increase your anticipation of heaven?

What other concerns does the reality of hell bring to your heart and mind?

The phrase "you will be like him" came up frequently in today's devotional reading. How does that promise make you feel?

HEARING
John 14:1–3 NIV:

> "Do not let your hearts be troubled. Trust in God; trust also in me. In my Father's house are many rooms; if it were not so, I would have told you. I am going there to prepare a place for you. And if I go and prepare a place for you, I will come back and take you to be with me that you also may be where I am."

REFLECTING
Jesus said these words only hours before he was nailed to the cross. Even then, how was he encouraging a forward-looking celebration?

What exciting dimension does Jesus add beyond the promise we have elsewhere—that we will be "like him"?

If the prevailing sounds of hell will be "weeping and gnashing of teeth," what do you think will be the prevailing sounds of heaven?

SPEAKING

What songs or hymns do you know by heart that seem to convey some of the excitement, worship, and celebration of heaven? Use one of them in a brief, personal recital of praise to God as you look forward to being like his Son.

What is it about the character of Jesus that you think you will enjoy sharing the most? How could you practice that trait in a small way for someone else today?

So we have stopped evaluating others by what the world thinks about them. Once I mistakenly thought of Christ that way, as though he were merely a human being. How differently I think about him now! What this means is that those who become Christians become new persons. They are not the same anymore, for the old life is gone. A new life has begun!
—2 Corinthians 5:16–17 NLT

Heavenly Heart

*C*an you see now why the angels rejoice when one sinner repents? Jesus knows what awaits the saved. He also knows what awaits the condemned. Can you see why we should rejoice as well? How can we? How can our hearts be changed so we rejoice as Jesus rejoices?

Ask God to help you have his eternal view of the world. His view of humanity is starkly simple. From his perspective every person is either:

- entering through the small gate or the wide gate (Matt. 7:11–14)
- traveling the narrow road or the wide road (Matt. 7:13, 14)
- building on rock or sand (Matt. 7:24–27)
- wise or foolish (Matt. 25:2)
- prepared or unprepared (Matt. 24:45–51)

▶ fruitful or fruitless (Matt. 25:14–27)
▶ heaven-called or hell-bound (Mark 16:15–16)

At the sinking of the RMS *Titanic*, over twenty-two hundred people were cast into the frigid waters of the Atlantic. On shore the names of the passengers were posted in two simple columns—saved and lost.*

God's list is equally simple.

Our ledger, however, is cluttered with unnecessary columns. Is he rich? Is she pretty? What work does he do? What color is her skin? Does she have a college degree? These matters are irrelevant to God. As he shapes us more and more to be like Jesus, they become irrelevant to us as well. "Our knowledge of men can no longer be based on their outward lives" (2 Cor. 5:16 PHILLIPS).

To have a heart like his is to look into the faces of the saved and rejoice! They are just one grave away from being just like Jesus. To have a heart like his is to look into the faces of the lost and pray. For unless they turn, they are one grave away from torment.

C. S. Lewis stated it this way:

It is a serious thing to live in a society of possible gods and goddesses, to remember that the dullest and most uninteresting person you talk to may one day be a creature which, if you saw it now, you would be strongly tempted to worship, or else a horror and a corruption such as now you meet only in a nightmare. All day

---

* James Ryle, unpublished manuscript. Used by permission

long we are, in some degree, helping each other to one or the other of these destinations.*

And so my challenge to you is simple. Ask God to help you have his eternal view of the world. Every person you meet has been given an invitation to dinner. When one says yes, celebrate! And when one acts sluggish as I did the night of my birthday, do what my daughters did. Stir him up and urge him to get ready. It's almost time for the party, and you don't want him to miss it.

THINKING
What was your gut reaction to C. S. Lewis's description of us as "possible gods and goddesses"?

How do you respond when you encounter someone who appears to be lost spiritually?

What person in the past year has done the most to help you along to your heavenly destination? What did they do?

---

* C. S. Lewis, *The Weight of Glory* (New York: Macmillan, 1949), 14–15.

HEARING

Revelation 21:3–4 NIV:

> And I heard a loud voice from the throne saying, "Now the dwelling of God is with men, and he will live with them. They will be his people, and God himself will be with them and be their God. He will wipe every tear from their eyes. There will be no more death or mourning or crying or pain, for the old order of things has passed away."

REFLECTING

When you read a passage like the one above, do you imagine someone saying this to you? Whose voice do you hear?

The passage lists a number of things that will not be part of heavenly life. Which of those hardships do you think you'll miss the least?

Are you stirred up and positively looking forward to the party, or are you still dragging your feet, not quite sure what surprise awaits you?

SPEAKING

Follow through on the challenge to ask God to help you have his eternal view of the world.

Take some time to pray for those in your life who are still on the "lost list." Ask the Lord to show you any ways you might influence their decisions.

Let us run the race that is before us and never give up.
—Hebrews 12:1

The Heart of a Runner

*H*ad golf existed in the New Testament era, I'm sure the writers would have spoken of mulligans and foot wedges, but it didn't, so they wrote about running. The word *race* is from the Greek *agon*, from which we get the word *agony*. The Christian's race is not a jog but rather a demanding and grueling, sometimes agonizing race. It takes a massive effort to finish strong.

Likely you've noticed that many don't. Surely you've observed there are many on the side of the trail. They used to be running. There was a time when they kept the pace. But then weariness set in. They didn't think the run would be this tough. Or they were discouraged by a bump and daunted by a fellow runner. Whatever the reason, they don't run anymore. They may be Christians. They may come to church. They may put a buck in the plate and warm a pew, but their hearts aren't in the race. They retired before their time. Unless something changes, their best work will have been their first work, and they will finish with a whimper.

By contrast, Jesus' best work was his final work, and his strongest step was his last step. Our Master is the classic example of one who endured. The writer of Hebrews went on to say that Jesus "held on while wicked people were doing evil things to him" (Hebrews 12:3). The Bible says Jesus "held on," implying that Jesus could have let go. The runner could have given up, sat down, gone home. He could have quit the race. But he didn't. "He held on while wicked people were doing evil things to him."

The Resistance

Have you ever thought about the evil things done to Christ? Can you think of times when Jesus could have given up? How about his time of temptation? You and I know what it is like to endure a moment of temptation or an hour of temptation, even a day of temptation. But *forty* days? That is what Jesus faced. "The Spirit led Jesus into the desert where the devil tempted Jesus for forty days" (Luke 4:1–2).

We imagine the wilderness temptation as three isolated events scattered over a forty-day period. Would that it had been. In reality, Jesus' time of testing was nonstop: "the devil tempted Jesus for forty days." Satan got on Jesus like a shirt and refused to leave. Every step, whispering in his ear. Every turn of the path, sowing doubt. Was Jesus impacted by the devil? Apparently so. Luke doesn't say that Satan *tried* to tempt Jesus. The verse doesn't read, the devil *attempted* to tempt Jesus. No the passage is clear: "the devil *tempted* Jesus." Jesus was *tempted*. He was tested. Tempted to change sides? Tempted to go home? Tempted to settle for a kingdom on earth? I don't know, but I know he was tempted. A war raged within. Stress stormed without. And since he was tempted, he could have quit the race. But he didn't. He kept on running.

Temptation didn't stop him, nor did accusations. Can

you imagine what it would be like to run in a race and be criticized by the bystanders?

Some years ago I entered a 5K race. Nothing serious, just a jog through the neighborhood to raise funds for a charity. Not being the wisest of runners, I started off at an impossible pace. Within a mile I was sucking air. At the right time, however, the spectators encouraged me. Sympathetic onlookers urged me on. One compassionate lady passed out cups of water; another sprayed us down with a hose. I had never seen these people, but that didn't matter. I needed a voice of encouragement, and they gave it. Bolstered by their assurance, I kept going.

What if, in the toughest steps of the race, I had heard words of accusation and not encouragement? And what if the accusations came not from strangers I could dismiss but from my neighbors and family?

How would you like somebody to yell these words at you as you ran?

"Hey, liar! Why don't you do something honest with your life?" (see John 7:12).

"Here comes the foreigner. Why don't you go home where you belong?" (see John 8:48).

"Since when do they let children of the devil enter the race?" (see John 8:48).

That's what happened to Jesus. His own family called him a lunatic. His neighbors treated him even worse. When Jesus returned to his hometown, they tried to throw him off a cliff (Luke 4:29). But Jesus didn't quit running. Temptations didn't deter him. Accusations didn't defeat him. Nor did shame dishearten him.

I invite you to think carefully about the supreme test Jesus faced in the race. Hebrews 12:2 offers this intriguing statement: "Jesus . . . accepted the shame as if it were nothing."

Shame is a feeling of disgrace, embarrassment, humiliation. Forgive me for stirring the memory, but don't you have a shameful moment in your history? Can you imagine the horror you would feel if everyone knew about it? What if a videotape of that event were played before your family and friends? How would you feel?

That is exactly what Jesus felt. *Why?* you ask. *He never did anything worthy of shame.* No, but we did. And since on the cross God made him become sin (2 Cor. 5:21), Jesus was covered with shame. He was shamed before his family. Stripped naked before his own mother and loved ones. Shamed before his fellow men. Forced to carry a cross until the weight caused him to stumble. Shamed before his church. The pastors and elders of his day mocked him, calling him names. Shamed before the city of Jerusalem. Condemned to die a criminal's death. Parents likely pointed to him from a distance and told their children, "That's what they do to evil men."

But the shame before men didn't compare with the shame Jesus felt before his Father. Our individual shame seems too much to bear. Can you imagine bearing the collective shame of all humanity? One wave of shame after another was dumped on Jesus. Though he never cheated, he was convicted as a cheat. Though he never stole, heaven regarded him as a thief. Though he never lied, he was considered a liar. Though he never lusted, he bore the shame of an adulterer. Though he always believed, he endured the disgrace of an infidel.

Such words stir one urgent question: How? How did he endure such disgrace? What gave Jesus the strength to endure the shame of the entire world? We need an answer, don't we? Like Jesus, we are tempted. Like Jesus, we are accused. Like Jesus, we are ashamed. But unlike Jesus, we give up. We give out. We sit down. How can we keep running as Jesus did? How can our hearts have the endurance Jesus had?

By focusing where Jesus focused: on "the joy that God put before him" (Heb. 12:2). Tomorrow we will look at Jesus' approach in detail. Today, let's think about what he faced.

THINKING

Which of Jesus' obstacles and resistance did you find resonating in some way with your own experiences in life?

In what ways were you able to identify with the story about running the race and being encouraged by strangers?

What would you say is the one thing you look forward to receiving when you consider undertaking a difficult task? What usually gives you joy at the end?

HEARING

Hebrews 12:1–3 NIV:

> Therefore, since we are surrounded by such a great cloud of witnesses, let us throw off everything that hinders and the sin that so easily entangles, and let us run with perseverance the race marked out for us. Let us fix our eyes on Jesus, the author and perfecter of our faith, who for the joy set before him endured the cross, scorning its shame, and sat down at the right hand of the throne of God.
>
> Consider him who endured such opposition from sinful men, so that you will not grow weary and lose heart.

REFLECTING

What phrases in this passage make the strongest impression on you in reading the verses together?

What other believers (dead and living) do you see in your cheering section, pulling for you to finish your race?

Based on this passage, what do you need to do in order to avoid "growing weary and losing heart"?

SPEAKING

Search out someone who had an impact on your spiritual life sometime earlier. Tell them you haven't forgotten and that you appreciate how the Lord used them in your life.

Spend some time in prayer, focused on the closing idea of the passage you just read. Perhaps begin the prayer, "Lord, for the next few minutes I want to consider you, your life, your teaching, your example to me, and your death for me."

Let us fix our eyes on Jesus, the author and perfecter of our faith, who for the joy set before him endured the cross, scorning its shame, and sat down at the right hand of the throne of God.
—Hebrews 12:2 NIV

The Gratified Heart

This verse above may very well be the greatest testimony ever written about the glory of heaven. Nothing is said about golden streets or angels' wings. No reference is made to music or feasts. Even the word *heaven* is missing from the verse. But though the word is missing, the power is not.

Remember, heaven was not foreign to Jesus. He is the only person to live on earth *after* he had lived in heaven. As believers, you and I will live in heaven after our time on earth, but Jesus did just the opposite. He knew heaven before he came to earth. He knew what awaited him upon his return. And knowing what awaited him in heaven enabled him to bear the shame on earth.

He "accepted the shame as if it were nothing because of the joy that God put before him" (Heb. 12:2). In his final moments, Jesus focused on the joy God put before him. He focused on the prize of heaven. By focusing on the prize, he was able not only to finish the race but to finish it strong.

I'm doing my best to do the same. In a far less significant ordeal, I, too, am seeking to finish strong. You are reading one of the last devotional thoughts of this book. I've lived with these pages: crafting thoughts, grooming paragraphs, pursuing the better verb, and digging for stronger conclusions. And now, the end is in sight.

Writing a book is much like running a long race. There is the initial burst of enthusiasm. Then the sags of energy. You give serious thought to giving up, but then a chapter will surprise you with a downhill slope. Occasionally an idea will inspire you. Often a chapter will tire you—not to mention those endless revisions demanded by relentless editors. But most of the work has the rhythm of a long-distance runner: long, sometimes lonely stretches at a steady pace.

And toward the end, with the finish line in sight and the editors content, there comes a numbing of the senses. You want to finish strong. You reach deep for the intensity you had months earlier, but the supply is scarce. The words blur, the illustrations run together, and the mind numbs. You need a kick, you need a surge, you need inspiration.

May I tell you where I find it? (This may sound peculiar, but bear with me.) Through years of writing at least one book a year, I've developed a ritual. Upon the completion of a project I enjoy a rite of celebration. I'm not into champagne, and I gave up cigars, but I have found something even sweeter. It involves two phases.

The first is a quiet moment before God. The moment the manuscript is in the mail, I find a secluded spot and stop. I don't say much, and, at least so far, neither does God. The purpose is not to talk as much as it is to relish. To delight in the sweet satisfaction of a completed task. Does a finer feeling exist? The runner feels the tape against his chest. It is finished. How sweet is the wine at the end of the journey. So for a few moments, God and I savor it together. We place the flag on the peak of Everest and enjoy the view.

Then (this really sounds mundane), I eat. I tend to skip meals during the homestretch, so I'm hungry. One year it was a Mexican dinner on the San Antonio River. Another it was room service and a basketball game. Last year I had catfish at a roadside café. Sometimes Denalyn joins me; other times I eat alone. The food may vary, and the company may change, but one rule remains constant. Throughout the meal I allow myself only one thought: *I am finished*. Planning future projects is not permitted. Consideration of tomorrow's tasks is not allowed. I indulge myself in a make-believe world and pretend that my life's work is complete.

And during that meal, in a minute way, I understand where Jesus found his strength. He lifted his eyes beyond the horizon and saw the table. He focused on the feast. And what he saw gave him strength to finish—and finish strong.

Such a moment awaits us. In a world oblivious to power abs and speed-reading, we'll take our place at the table. In an hour that has no end, we will rest. Surrounded by saints and engulfed by Jesus himself, we will know the work is, indeed, finished. The final harvest will have been gathered, we will be seated, and Christ will christen the meal with these words: "Well done, good and faithful servant" (Matt. 25:23 KJV).

And in that moment, the race will have been worth it.

THINKING
What intense feelings do you connect with the experience of finishing a project or effort?

When you've heard about that salute that Jesus wants to give you, "Well done, good and faithful servant," what have you thought might be your response to such an honor?

As you near the end of this book, what has your heart discovered it will need to finish the race of life and finish it strong?

HEARING
1 Timothy 4:15–16 NIV:

> Be diligent in these matters; give yourself wholly to them, so that everyone may see your progress. Watch your life and doctrine closely. Persevere in them, because if you do, you will save both yourself and your hearers.

REFLECTING
Every finish involves delayed gratification. What have been your greatest personal victories in finishing well?

The word *progress* plays a key role in the verses above. Whether running a race or carrying out a great task, progress eventually leads to the finish. How would you measure your present progress in running the race set before you by Christ?

Just as the writer approaches the end of his book effort, you're approaching the end of your task of reading and thinking and meditating. What are some long-term concerns about your life as a believer that you want to watch closely in the years to come in order to make progress and finish strong?

SPEAKING

Make it a point to encourage at least one other believer in the next few days. Think about the ways in which you have seen progress in his or her faith-race, and tell that person how that progress has encouraged you to keep running.

Thank the Lord for those times when you've been tempted to veer from the track but the Holy Spirit managed to get your attention directly, or through another believer, just enough to keep you going in the race. Express your anticipation about the finish line.

I pray that your hearts will be flooded with light so that you can understand the wonderful future he has promised to those he called. I want you to realize what a rich and glorious inheritance he has given to his people.
—Ephesians 1:18 NLT

A Heart Fixed on Jesus

There are times when we see. And there are times when we see. Let me show you what I mean:

Everything changes the morning you see the For Sale sign on your neighbor's boat. His deluxe bass boat. The bass boat you've coveted for three summers. All of a sudden nothing else matters. A gravitational tug pulls your car to the curb. You sigh as you behold your dream glistening in the sun. You run your fingers along the edge, pausing only to wipe the drool from your shirt. As you gaze, you are transported to Lake Tamapwantee, and it's just you and the glassy waters and your bass boat.

Or perhaps the following paragraph describes you better:

Everything changes the day you see him enter the English lit classroom. Just enough swagger to be cool.

Just enough smarts to be classy. Not walking so fast
as to be nervous or so slow as to be cocky. You've seen
him before but only in your dreams. Now he's really
here. And you can't take your eyes off him. By the
time class is over, you've memorized every curl and
lash. And by the time this day is over, you resolve he's
going to be yours.

There are times when we see. And then there are times
when we *see*. There are times when we observe, and there are
times when we memorize. There are times when we notice,
and there are times when we study. Most of us know what it
means to see a new boat or a new boy . . . but do we know
what it's like to see Jesus? Do we know what it's like to "fix
our eyes on Jesus" (Heb. 12:2 NIV)?

We've spent the last twenty-eight days looking at what
it means to be just like Jesus. The world has never known a
heart so pure, a character so flawless. His spiritual bearing
was so keen he never missed a heavenly whisper. His mercy so
abundant he never missed a chance to forgive. No lie left his
lips; no distraction marred his vision. He touched when others
recoiled. He endured when others quit. Jesus is the ultimate
model for every person. And what we have done in these pages
is precisely what God invites you to do with the rest of your
life. He urges you to fix your eyes upon Jesus. Heaven invites
you to set the lens of your heart on the heart of the Savior and
make him the object of your life. For that reason, I want us to
close our time together with this question: What does it mean
to *see* Jesus?

The shepherds can tell us. For them it wasn't enough to
see the angels. You'd think it would have been. Night sky

shattered with light. Stillness erupting with song. Simple shepherds roused from their sleep and raised to their feet by a choir of angels: "Glory to God in the highest!" Never had these men seen such splendor.

But it wasn't enough to see the angels. The shepherds wanted to see the one who sent the angels. Since they wouldn't be satisfied until they saw him, you can trace the long line of Jesus-seekers to a person of the pasture who said, "Let's go. . . . Let's *see*" (Luke 2:15, emphasis mine).

Not far behind the shepherds was a man named Simeon. Luke tells us Simeon was a good man who served in the temple during the time of Christ's birth. Luke also tells us, "Simeon had been told by the Holy Spirit that he would not die before he saw the Christ promised by the Lord" (Luke 2:26). This prophecy was fulfilled only a few days after the shepherds saw Jesus. Somehow Simeon knew that the blanketed bundle he saw in Mary's arms was the almighty God. And for Simeon, seeing Jesus was enough. Now he was ready to die. Some don't want to die until they've seen the world. Simeon's dream was not so timid. He didn't want to die until he had seen the maker of the world. He had to see Jesus.

He prayed: "God, you can now release your servant; release me in peace as you promised. With *my own eyes* I've seen your salvation" (Luke 2:29–30 MSG, emphasis mine).

The Magi had the same desire. Like Simeon, they wanted to see Jesus. Like the shepherds, they were not satisfied with what they saw in the night sky. Not that the star wasn't spectacular. Not that the star wasn't historical. To be a witness of the blazing orb was a privilege, but for the Magi, it wasn't enough. It wasn't enough to see the light over Bethlehem; they had to see the Light of Bethlehem. It was him they came to see.

And they succeeded! They all succeeded. More remarkable than their diligence was Jesus' willingness. Jesus wanted to be seen! Whether they came from the pasture or the palace, whether they lived in the temple or among the sheep, whether their gift was of gold or honest surprise . . . they were welcomed. Search for one example of one person who desired to see the infant Jesus and was turned away. You won't find it.

You will find examples of those who didn't seek him. Those, like King Herod, who were content with less. Those, like the religious leaders, who preferred to read about him than to see him. The ratio between those who missed him and those who sought him was thousands to one. But the ratio between those who sought him and those who found him was one to one. *All who sought him found him.* Long before the words were written, this promise was proven: "God . . . rewards those who truly want to find him" (Heb. 11:6).

The examples continue. Consider John and Andrew. They, too, were rewarded. For them it wasn't enough to listen to John the Baptist. Most would have been content to serve in the shadow of the world's most famous evangelist. Could there be a better teacher? Only one. And when John and Andrew saw him, they left John the Baptist and followed Jesus. Note the request they made.

"They said, 'Rabbi, where are you staying?'" (John 1:38). Pretty bold request. They didn't ask Jesus to give them a minute or an opinion or a message or a miracle. They asked for his address. They wanted to hang out with him. They wanted to know him. They wanted to know what caused his head to turn and his heart to burn and his soul to yearn. They wanted to study his eyes and follow his steps. They wanted to see him. They wanted to know what made him laugh and if he ever got tired. And most of all, they wanted to know, *Could Jesus be who John said he was—and if he is, what on earth is God doing on the earth?* You can't answer such a question by talking to his cousin; you've got to talk to the man himself.

Jesus' answer to the disciples? "Come and see" (v. 39). He didn't say, "Come and glance," or "Come and peek." He said, "Come and see." Bring your bifocals and binoculars. This is no time for side-glances or occasional peeks. "Let us fix our eyes on Jesus, the author and perfecter of our faith" (Heb. 12:2 NIV).

The fisherman fixes his eyes on the boat. The girl fixes her eyes on the boy. The disciple fixes his eyes on the Savior.

That's what Matthew did. Matthew, if you remember, was converted at work. According to his résumé, he was a revenue consultant for the government. According to his neighbors, he was a crook. He kept a tax booth and a hand extended at the street corner. That's where he was the day he saw Jesus. "Follow me," the Master said, and Matthew did. And in the very next verse we find Jesus sitting at Matthew's dining room table. "Jesus was having dinner at Matthew's house" (Matt. 9:10).

A curbside conversion couldn't satisfy his heart, so Matthew took Jesus home. Something happens over a dinner table that doesn't happen over an office desk. Take off the tie, heat up the grill, break out the sodas, and spend the evening with the suspender of the stars. "You know, Jesus, forgive me for asking but I've always wanted to know . . ."

THINKING

What's the first thing you see when you fix your eyes on Jesus?

156

How have you personally experienced the truth of the verse, "God . . . rewards those who truly want to find him" (Heb. 11:6)?

Thinking about the illustration of Matthew above, what would be several topics of conversation that you would want to have with Jesus?

HEARING
Luke 24:13–17, 27–32 NIV:

> Now that same day two of them were going to a village called Emmaus, about seven miles from Jerusalem. They were talking with each other about everything that had happened. As they talked and discussed these things with each other, Jesus himself came up and walked along with them; but they were kept from recognizing him.
>
> He asked them, "What are you discussing together as you walk along?" They stood still, their faces downcast.
>
> And beginning with Moses and all the Prophets, he explained to them what was said in all the Scriptures concerning himself.
>
> As they approached the village to which they were going, Jesus acted as if he were going farther. But they urged him strongly, "Stay with us, for it is

nearly evening; the day is almost over." So he went in to stay with them.

When he was at the table with them, he took bread, gave thanks, broke it and began to give it to them. Then their eyes were opened and they recognized him, and he disappeared from their sight. They asked each other, "Were not our hearts burning within us while he talked with us on the road and opened the Scriptures to us?"

REFLECTING
Why do you want to spend time with Jesus? What effect does his presence have on you?

At what points in your Christian experience have you felt something like those two disciples reported after the Emmaus walk, "our hearts burning within us"?

SPEAKING
Thank the Lord for all the times he has tracked you down in life and allowed you the joy of discovering that he was walking right beside you along the way.

What are some times and places that you have been taking for granted (like church) where you can express to Jesus your intent of enjoying his company?

But without faith it is impossible to please him: for he
that cometh to God must believe that he is, and that
he is a rewarder of them that diligently seek him.
—Hebrews 11:6 KJV

The Heart Jesus Enters

*W*e ended yesterday's thoughts with Matthew taking Jesus home for a dinner party. Though Matthew giving Jesus his invitation is impressive, the acceptance is more so. Didn't matter to Jesus that Matthew was a thief. Didn't matter to Jesus that Matthew had built a split-level house with the proceeds of extortion. What did matter was that Matthew wanted to know Jesus, and since God "rewards those who truly want to find him" (Heb. 11:6), Matthew was rewarded with the presence of Christ in his home.

Of course, it only made sense that Jesus would spend time with Matthew. After all, Matthew was a top draft pick, shoulder-tapped to write the first book of the New Testament. Jesus hangs out with only the big guys like Matthew and Andrew and John. Right?

May I counter that opinion with an example? Zacchaeus was far from a big guy. He was small—so small he couldn't see over the crowd that lined the street the day Jesus came to Jericho. Of course the crowd might have let him elbow up to the front, except that he, like Matthew, was a tax collector. But he, like Matthew, had a hunger in his heart to see Jesus.

It wasn't enough to stand at the back of the crowd. It wasn't enough to peer through a cardboard telescope. It wasn't enough to listen to someone else describe the parade of the Messiah. Zacchaeus wanted to see Jesus with his own eyes.

So he went out on a limb. Clad in a three-piece Armani suit and brand-new Italian loafers, he shimmied up a tree in hopes of seeing Christ.

I wonder if you would be willing to do the same. Would you go out on a limb to see Jesus? Not everyone would. In the same Bible where we read about Zacchaeus crawling across the limb, we read about a young ruler. Unlike Zacchaeus, the crowd parted to make room for him. He was the . . . ahem . . . *rich* young ruler. Upon learning that Jesus was in the area, he called for the limo, cruised across town, and approached the carpenter. Please note the question he had for Jesus: "Teacher, what good thing must I do to have life forever?" (Matt. 19:16).

Bottom-line sort of fellow, this ruler. No time for formalities or conversations. "Let's get right to the issue. Your schedule is busy; so is mine. Tell me how I can get saved, and I'll leave you alone."

There was nothing wrong with his question, but there was a problem with his heart. Contrast his desire with that of Zacchaeus, "Can I make it up that tree?"

Or John and Andrew, "Where are you staying?"

Or Matthew, "Can you spend the evening?"

Or Simeon, "Can I stay alive until I see him?"

Or the Magi, "Saddle up the camels. We aren't stopping until we find him."

Or the shepherds, "Let's go. . . . Let's see."

See the difference? The rich young ruler wanted medicine. The others wanted the Physician. The ruler wanted an answer to the quiz. They wanted the Teacher. He was in a hurry. They had all the time in the world. He settled for a cup of coffee at the drive-through window. They wouldn't settle for anything less than a full-course meal at the banquet table. They wanted more than salvation. They wanted the Savior. They wanted to see Jesus.

They were earnest in their search. One translation renders Hebrews 11:6: "God . . . rewards those who *earnestly* seek him" (NIV, emphasis mine).

And another: "God . . . rewards those who *sincerely look* for him" (TLB, emphasis mine).

I like the King James translation: "He is a rewarder of them that *diligently* seek him" (emphasis mine).

Diligently—what a great word. Be diligent in your search. Be hungry in your quest, relentless in your pilgrimage. Let this book be but one of dozens you read about Jesus and this hour be but one of hundreds in which you seek him. Step away from the puny pursuits of possessions and positions, and seek your King.

Don't be satisfied with angels. Don't be content with stars in the sky. Seek him out as the shepherds did. Long for him as Simeon did. Worship him as the wise men did. Do as John and Andrew did: ask for his address. Do as Matthew: invite Jesus into your house. Imitate Zacchaeus. Risk whatever it takes to see Christ.

God rewards those who seek *him*. Not those who seek doctrine or religion or systems or creeds. Many settle for these lesser passions, but the reward goes to those who settle for nothing less than Jesus himself. And what is the reward?

What awaits those who seek Jesus? Nothing short of the heart of Jesus. "And as the Spirit of the Lord works within us, we become more and more like him" (2 Cor. 3:18 TLB).

Can you think of a greater gift than to be like Jesus? Christ felt no guilt; God wants to banish yours. Jesus had no bad habits; God wants to remove yours. Jesus had no fear of death; God wants you to be fearless. Jesus had kindness for the diseased and mercy for the rebellious and courage for the challenges. God wants you to have the same.

He loves you just the way you are, but he refuses to leave you that way. He wants you to be just like Jesus.

THINKING

Which of the versions of Hebrews 11:6 that were quoted plucked your heartstrings with a challenge: "earnestly," "search," "sincerely look," or "diligently seek"?

When was the last time you went out on a limb or even out of your way in hopes of spending time with Jesus?

What evidence indicates that the verse quoted above is true in your life, that "as the Spirit of the Lord works within [you], [you've] become more and more like him"?

HEARING

John 14:23:

> Jesus answered, "If people love me, they will obey
> my teaching. My Father will love them, and we will
> come to them and make our home with them."

REFLECTING

What three lasting impressions about the heartbeat of Jesus
have been left in your heart as you have experienced these
thirty days?

Which of the heroes from this last day's reading would you
like to be more like: Zacchaeus, John, Andrew, Simeon, the
Magi, or the shepherds of Bethlehem?

According to Jesus' statement above, we demonstrate love
for him by obedience. What new area of obedience could
you undertake as an expression of love for him?

SPEAKING

Flip back through the titles of the various daily devotions as you spend some time praying about the development of your heart. As the titles strike a responsive chord, ask the Lord to bring out that trait of Jesus' heart in yours.

The following is one of Paul's prayers for the Ephesian Christians. As you read it, make it your own:

> And I pray that Christ will be more and more at home in your hearts as you trust in him. May your roots go down deep into the soil of God's marvelous love. And may you have the power to understand, as all God's people should, how wide, how long, how high, and how deep his love really is. May you experience the love of Christ, though it is so great you will never fully understand it. Then you will be filled with the fullness of life and power that comes from God. (Eph. 3:17–19 NLT)

The Lucado Reader's Guide

Discover . . . Inside every book by Max Lucado, you'll find words of encouragement and inspiration that will draw you into a deeper experience with Jesus and treasures for your walk with God. What will you discover?

3:16: The Numbers of Hope
. . . the 26 words that can change your life.
core scripture: John 3:16

And the Angels Were Silent
. . . what Jesus Christ's final days can teach you about what matters most.
core scripture: Matthew 20–27

The Applause of Heaven
. . . the secret to a truly satisfying life.
core scripture: The Beatitudes, Matthew 5:1–10

Come Thirsty
. . . how to rehydrate your heart and sink into the wellspring of God's love.
core scripture: John 7:37–38

Cure for the Common Life
. . . the unique things God designed you to do with your life.
core scripture: 1 Corinthians 12:7

Facing Your Giants
. . . when God is for you, no challenge is too great.
core scripture: 1 and 2 Samuel

Fearless
. . . how faith is the antidote to the fear in your life.
core scripture: John 14:1, 3

A Gentle Thunder
. . . the God who will do whatever it takes to lead his children back to him.
core scripture: Psalm 81:7

Great Day, Every Day
. . . how living in a purposeful way will help you trust more, stress less.
core scripture: Psalm 118:24

The Great House of God
. . . a blueprint for peace, joy, and love found in the Lord's Prayer.
core scripture: The Lord's Prayer, Matthew 6:9–13

God Came Near
. . . a love so great that it left heaven to become part of your world.
core scripture: John 1:14

He Chose the Nails
. . . a love so deep that it chose death on a cross—just to win your heart.
core scripture: 1 Peter 1:18–20

He Still Moves Stones
. . . the God who still does the impossible—in your life.
core scripture: Matthew 12:20

In the Eye of the Storm
. . . peace in the storms of your life.
core scripture: John 6

In the Grip of Grace
. . . the greatest gift of all—the grace of God.
core scripture: Romans

It's Not About Me
. . . why focusing on God will make sense of your life.
core scripture: 2 Corinthians 3:18

Just Like Jesus
. . . a life free from guilt, fear, and anxiety.
core scripture: Ephesians 4:23–24

A Love Worth Giving
. . . how living loved frees you to love others.
core scripture: 1 Corinthians 13

Next Door Savior
. . . a God who walked life's hardest trials—and still walks with you through yours.
core scripture: Matthew 16:13–16

No Wonder They Call Him the Savior
. . . hope in the unlikeliest place—upon the cross.
core scripture: Romans 5:15

Outlive Your Life
. . . that a great God created you to do great things.
core scripture: Acts 1

Six Hours One Friday
. . . forgiveness and healing in the middle of loss and failure.
core scripture: John 19–20

Traveling Light
. . . the power to release the burdens you were never meant to carry.
core scripture: Psalm 23

When God Whispers Your Name
. . . the path to hope in knowing that God knows you, never forgets you, and cares about the details of your life.
core scripture: John 10:3

When Christ Comes
. . . why the best is yet to come.
core scripture: 1 Corinthians 15:23

Recommended reading if you're struggling with . . .

FEAR AND WORRY

Come Thirsty
Fearless
For the Tough Times
Next Door Savior
Traveling Light

DISCOURAGEMENT

He Still Moves Stones
Next Door Savior

GRIEF/DEATH OF A LOVED ONE

Next Door Savior
Traveling Light
When Christ Comes
When God Whispers Your Name

GUILT

In the Grip of Grace
Just Like Jesus

LONELINESS

God Came Near

SIN

Facing Your Giants
He Chose the Nails
Six Hours One Friday

WEARINESS

When God Whispers Your Name

Recommended reading if you want to know more about . . .

THE CROSS

And the Angels Were Silent
He Chose the Nails
No Wonder They Call Him the Savior
Six Hours One Friday

GRACE

He Chose the Nails
In the Grip of Grace

HEAVEN

The Applause of Heaven
When Christ Comes

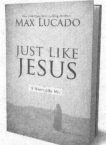

SHARING THE GOSPEL

God Came Near
No Wonder They Call Him the Savior

Recommended reading if you're looking for more . . .

COMFORT

For the Tough Times
He Chose the Nails
Next Door Savior
Traveling Light

COMPASSION

Outlive Your Life

COURAGE

Facing Your Giants
Fearless

HOPE

3:16: The Numbers of Hope
Facing Your Giants
A Gentle Thunder
God Came Near

JOY

The Applause of Heaven
Cure for the Common Life
When God Whispers Your Name

LOVE

Come Thirsty
A Love Worth Giving
No Wonder They Call Him the Savior

PEACE

And the Angels Were Silent
The Great House of God
In the Eye of the Storm
Traveling Light

SATISFACTION

And the Angels Were Silent
Come Thirsty
Cure for the Common Life
Great Day, Every Day

TRUST

A Gentle Thunder
It's Not About Me
Next Door Savior

Max Lucado books make great gifts!

If you're coming up to a special occasion, consider one of these.

FOR ADULTS:

For the Tough Times
Grace for the Moment
Live Loved
The Lucado Life Lessons Study Bible
Mocha with Max
DaySpring Daybrighteners® and cards

FOR TEENS/GRADUATES:

Let the Journey Begin
You Can Be Everything God Wants You to Be
You Were Made to Make a Difference

FOR KIDS:

Just in Case You Ever Wonder
The Oak Inside the Acorn
You Are Special

FOR PASTORS AND TEACHERS:

God Thinks You're Wonderful
You Changed My Life

AT CHRISTMAS:

The Crippled Lamb
Christmas Stories from Max Lucado
God Came Near